Shelby's Horse-Filled Summer:

An Old Quarry Lake Farms Tale

Marty Kay Jones

Copyright ©2023 by Marty Kay Jones

All rights reserved.

No part of this publication may be reproduced, distributed, or transmitted in any form or by any means, including photocopying, recording, or other electronic or mechanical methods, without the prior written permission of the publisher, except as permitted by U.S. copyright law. For permission requests, contact Marty Kay Jones.

The story, all names, characters, and incidents portrayed in this production are fictitious. No identification with actual persons (living or deceased), places, buildings, and products is intended or should be inferred.

Book Cover by Lucia Benito

Contents

Download The Audio Version of This Book for Free!	V
About The Author	VII
Exclusive Old Quarry Lake Farms Insider Info	VIII
1. The Summer of the Horse	1
2. The Great Camp Debate	13
3. Placement Testing	26
4. The Results Are In	42
5. The Opposite of Shopping	54
6. First Day of Camp Blues	64
7. Camp Days Continue	75
8. Sit Up, Relax, and Ride	81
9. The Right Place at the Right Time!	92
10. Whisper the Magic Pony	102
11. Saying Farewell to the Summer	111
Glossary	116
Review	138

Exclusive Old Quarry Lake Farms Insider Info	139
Please join My Facebook group	141

Download The Audio Version of This Book for Free!

If you love listening to audiobooks on the go or enjoy the narration as you read along I have great news for you.

You can download this book for FREE just by signing up for a FREE 30-day audible trial.

Scan this code to download it

About The Author

Like Old Quarry Lake's newest resident, Shelby Simone, author Marty Kay Jones grew up obsessed with horses. She also lived in the city and had to wait until her teen years to experience them for herself.

Today, Marty Kay Jones is still obsessed with horses, but now she gets to see them every day. She runs a small boarding stable in the Appalachian foothills and loves teaching new generations everything there is to know about horses.

Ms. Jones believes learning never stops and extends her equine knowledge to readers of the Old Quarry Lake Farms book series. While the books are written about 11-year-old Shelby Simone and her sixth-grade friends, readers of all ages will appreciate and identify with the challenges and triumphs that come with the major life changes Shelby experiences.

When not playing with her own horses, Chip and Mango, Ms. Jones can be found hiking with her Australian Sheep Dog Petey, tinkering around with her project hot rod, or curled up with a good mystery novel.

Exclusive Old Quarry Lake Farms Insider Info

Do you want to join Shelby Simone and her friends from Old Quarry Lake Farms on all their adventures?

Read about Shelby, Katherine, Rose, and all their pals in the Old Quarry Lake Farms Tales book series. Three girls who are wild about horses unite at their local town horse-riding stable. Together, they learn about horses, themselves, and what it means to be a good friend.

The Old Quarry Lake Farms Tales join a group of pre-teen girls who share a bond through horses. Together, they tackle situations like moving to a new town, feeling different, and accepting themselves and each other just as they are—while learning everything they can about horses!

Scan the code to join the Old Quarry Lake Farms email list and never miss out on Shelby's adventures. You'll gain access to bonus material, behind-the-scenes details, and sneak peeks at where Shelby's next steps will take her!

Chapter One

The Summer of the Horse

"No, but seriously. How do you not like macaroni and cheese?" Shelby Simone frowned, completely confused. How *did* somebody not like macaroni and cheese?

"It's not that I *don't* like it," her friend Rose Jensen tried to explain. "It's just that if there was literally anything else to choose from, I would probably choose that instead of mac 'n' cheese."

"So do you like any kind of pasta?" This third voice came from their friend Katherine Wilson, who was attempting to paint her fingernails while sitting at Shelby's desk. She tried to concentrate hard so she didn't splash nail polish everywhere. After all, it wasn't her desk.

"Yes!" Rose nodded excitedly. "I love pasta. I love my dad's marinara sauce, even though it's just the stuff from the jar with what he calls 'extra love.'" She rolled her eyes. Sheriff Jensen always seemed like such a no-nonsense man when serving the residents of Old Quarry Lake, but he was much jollier at home with Rose, her mom, and twin toddler siblings, Peony and Jacob.

Shelby's eyes lit up. "Ok, cool! Do you think you'd want to try my parents' marinara sauce? It's jar stuff too, but they add 'a little more culture' instead of 'extra love.' Dad says that learning how to season food is one of the anthropological markers for modern hominids."

Shelby's parents, Dr. and Mr. Simone, were anthropologists. Rose and Katherine were slowly getting used to some of the more interesting topics of conversation at the Simone house.

"What does that mean in regular people talk?" Rose asked jokingly.

Shelby and her father were always tossing out what Rose's dad, Sheriff Jensen, called ten-dollar words. Rose had to ask about that one, too, and her dad explained, "They use big words when little ones would be fine. But that's ok; we all probably need to remember how to speak right," he said this with a wink.

"Spices, Rose," Shelby said with a chuckle. "Dad seems to think that the difference between humans and early hominids is the way they use other plants and seeds to season their food. But as far as what Mom and Dad actually put in their spaghetti sauce, it's like, four shakes of a bottle of Italian seasoning and some garlic powder. It's not exactly super evolved."

Rose giggled, too. "Your dad might be right about the home whatsis, but it sounds like the recipe is basically the same as my dad's. I'd be happy to try your parents' sauce."

Shelby grinned widely. "Awesome. I'll let my mom know that spaghetti is cool for dinner. Is everyone good with breadsticks and a little salad? It's usually, like, lettuce, tomato, and croutons. Maybe some shredded cheese. Sound good?"

SHELBY'S HORSE-FILLED SUMMER: 3

Katherine and Rose agreed that a spaghetti dinner sounded delicious, and thanked Shelby again for inviting them for dinner. Shelby hurried down the stairs to share the results of the dinner discussion with her mother.

Katherine continued painting her nails, frowning with every careful stroke of the brush. Shelby was letting her borrow a metallic blue nail polish that looked bright and pretty against Katherine's dark skin. She wanted to do her best to not make a mess or waste any of Shelby's polish, so she was trying to absolutely and precisely dab the paint on her nails only.

Except... it wasn't going so well. Katherine couldn't remember when she'd polished her nails in recent history. After all, nail polish started to chip off pretty much the first time she went to the barn after using it, so why bother?

Katherine and Rose had met Shelby at Old Quarry Lake Farms, the horseback riding stable where the two of them boarded their horses. Though Katherine and Rose had grown up together, Shelby was a newcomer to riding horses and Old Quarry Lake.

As anthropologists at the Metropolitan Museum of History in the state capital, Dr. and Mr. Simone had come to Old Quarry Lake to help with a Native American archaeological site that had been uncovered recently. The site had been revealed when the town had begun construction on an expansion for the Old Quarry Lake School building, and now Shelby's parents and other team members were racing against the upcoming school schedule to stabilize and analyze the site. Given that the site was over two hours away from the downtown metro area, the Simone family had left the city for rural life.

Though Shelby was still adjusting to the day-to-day experience in what her father (and only her father) called The OQL, she was thrilled to have made friends with Katherine and Rose almost immediately. Despite them being respectfully terrified of horses, as Dr. Simone explained to the girls and their families, Shelby's parents had gifted her with two months of riding lessons at Old Quarry Lake Farms.

According to the collection of horse magazines and blogs that Shelby was subscribed to, Old Quarry Lake Farms was one of the best riding stables in the entire Midwest. The owner, Bill Radnor, was not only a big deal in the barrel world, but he opened his barn to trainers of all sorts of equine sports. That meant that riders could try out many different riding disciplines, from dressage and jumping to Western Pleasure and everything in between.

Katherine and Rose had been riding at Old Quarry Lake Farms "Since I was able to ask for a horsey," Rose had explained. The two girls had been in riding lessons together and even got their first horses around the same time. Katherine and her Quarter Horse mare Comet mostly worked on English equitation, meaning Katherine practiced her form and technique as she rode Comet through different patterns and gaits. Rose and her Thoroughbred gelding Whisper were daredevils and enjoyed jumping anything that stood in their way.

Since Shelby had just started riding a couple of weeks earlier, she didn't know what kind of riding she preferred. She knew that she wanted to try jumping, but for now, she was getting used to trotting on the lunge line and learning how to steer Coins, the big Appaloosa lesson horse, at a walk. Bill was a great teacher, and Shelby, who had been obsessed with horses since birth, was eager to learn.

After some early misunderstandings, the girls quickly became inseparable. Katherine and Rose not only helped Shelby learn more about horses but introduced her to the town of Old Quarry Lake and the people who lived there. Shelby felt like she was actually, kind of, maybe starting to fit in.

Tonight, the girls were gathered at the Simone household. Mr. Simone was stuck at the lab with some new samples that had been unearthed that day, so

Dr. Simone had picked up the girls from the barn. They planned to have dinner while watching the latest episode of *Swann Johnson: Teen Cowboy*.

Shelby didn't exactly love Swann Johnson. Whoever was working on the show got so many things wrong about horses. Still, Rose had an unwavering crush on Swann, and Katherine and Shelby's mom were weirdly obsessed with the plot line involving Swann and his evil stepmother, Cindy. They were sharing some of their wilder theories as they gathered around the coffee table in the den. Sitting on the floor to eat dinner in front of the TV was pretty normal in the Simone household, and the other girls loved this tradition.

"Ok, but when Cindy said, 'I know where you come from, Swann,' I know she was talking about Swann's birth mother Denise," Dr. Simone said. "Everyone knows Swann is from Sweden originally and moved to Texas as a baby."

"Well yeah," Katherine countered," but the rodeo promoters don't know that Swann's not a Texan. And if Cindy tells them that Swann is really Swedish, he'll get fired and he'll never be a big star with the rodeo."

"But that isn't logical! If he loses the endorsement, then the family will lose the Double Diamond ranch. Cindy would be ruined." Rose and Shelby sat silently, eyes wide. Shelby's mom blushed at her own outburst. With a grin, she gestured at the food. "Everyone get their garlic bread and salad, and we'll get started once everyone is ready."

For the next hour, the three girls and Dr. Simone followed the Johnson family through their adventures on the family ranch in Texas. As usual, the show ended in the middle of what might have been another clue about Cindy's plans. Shelby's mom and Katherine chatted about the new possibilities as Shelby and Rose cleared the plates and placed them in the dishwasher.

While the dishwasher hummed away, they pulled out a deck of cards for a game of Uno. Shelby's mom was generally considered unbeatable at Uno. She said she had played it constantly when she was completing her doctorate research in Guatemala. She'd even invented a form of Uno Solitaire while living in a tent in the rainforest. Naturally, Katherine and Rose were excited to have their own local Uno master to help them improve their games. Shelby's Uno game wavered between genius and questionable, but she enjoyed watching the others concentrating so hard on a card game.

Conversation faded away as the players focused on their strategies. After each round, they'd stretch, chat, get drinks, and use the restroom as needed, but when they were seated at the table, they barely spoke.

It was during one of the stretch breaks that Katherine mentioned horse camp. Dr. Simone was in the kitchen, slicing a log of grocery store cookie dough to bake for dessert.

"So, you know how Bill's doing an extra round of horse camp this year?" Katherine looked back and forth between Shelby and Rose, who were each performing some kind of table-side stretch on opposite sides of the den.

"Yeah," Rose said. "Since we're probably getting an extra-long summer with the school under construction."

"Right. But there's plenty of interest in it, too. He said the waitlist was long enough to make him offer another session."

"So, what about it?" Rose asked.

"I'm going to be a junior counselor," Katherine squealed.

"I knew it!" Rose shrieked back. "How did you do it? How did you just sit here all night like whatever, with that type of news?"

Katherine shrugged. "I actually just got a text from Bill during the last stretch break, but I had two Draw Four cards in the next hand, so I wanted to see how that played out first."

"Like you wouldn't lose magnificently to Shelby's mom, just like every other time?" Rose was beaming as she joked with her friend. No one won at Dr. Simone's Uno table except Dr. Simone... yet.

"Whatever," Katherine rolled her eyes and grinned at this true statement.

"Ok, so, Katherine, I'm really happy for you, but what are we even talking about?" Shelby asked innocently.

Katherine laughed. "Thank you, Shelby. I'm excited too." Then she explained, "The farm usually hosts a summer riding camp for kids of all different groups. It starts with Pre-Green, who are little kids who basically get pony rides and a little lesson about easy-to-understand horsey stuff for a few hours a day. Then there's the Green group, which is kids who can mostly sit on a horse by themselves but generally aren't older than, like, 8. Then Junior, which is kids our age." She pointed between the three of them as she took a big gulp of lemonade. "Then after that, you can go into the Amateur or teen groups or help out with the younger kids' camps, which is what I'm doing. I've already done two years of Junior, and I'm too young for Amateur," she clarified.

"The first horse camp happened before you moved here," Rose said. "I didn't actually sign up for camp, but since I'm *always* at the barn, I *always* seem to end up wrangling babies with the Pre-Green group." She put special emphasis on the word always but shrugged as she spoke. It did seem that Rose ended up helping people with their small children at the barn. Maybe it came easy to her to constantly help with her mother's daycare business.

"You should totally sign up for this camp," Katherine said, her eyes growing wide. "Drew could take us both each day," she said, referring to her brother, who often shuttled the girls back and forth from riding lessons. "Camp runs from 7:00 am to 5:30 pm every day for a week. Don't worry; they feed you lunch and snacks and stuff, or you can bring your own."

"What do you do all day?" Shelby was curious. Spending a full day in the presence of horses sounded glorious in any case, but she wanted to know what she was getting herself into.

Katherine frowned thoughtfully. "Well, you learn about the horse's body parts and ride—of course, you ride. Usually, you get to ride twice a day. But there are all sorts of lessons, not just body parts. We talked about all the different riding disciplines, and the trainers put on demonstrations. Sometimes we learn about different breeds, or how horses are used around the world."

That last bit really interested Shelby. After all, she had multicultural research in her genes. Then again, Katherine could have stopped at *ride twice a day*, and Shelby would have been sold.

She snapped back to reality. "But I thought you said it was full or whatever?"

Katherine shook her head. "Not quite. Bill had enough interested waitlist people, but not all of them could fit the second session into their summer schedule. What he said in his text was 'almost full', which means there's room for more."

Shelby frowned again. "I bet it's expensive, though. My parents probably wouldn't be into it."

"I have no idea," Katherine replied. "It's a different cost for me because I use my own horse. But you should totally check into it. It would be so much fun. Plus, you'd probably be put in the Junior group, and we could hang out at lunch when I'm not supervising the little guys!"

Shelby laughed, "I barely qualify for Pre-Green. I'm not even trotting off the lunge line yet."

Rose patted her on the back, "But you're getting there. Seriously. You've only had, what, four lessons? And you're already walking off the lunge line? That's really great!"

Shelby blushed a bright red. Rose was perfectly happy jumping what Shelby considered to be pretty big fences with Whisper. And here she was, congratulating Shelby on walking by herself—the most basic possible thing in horseback riding.

But Shelby knew Rose meant every word. If there was one thing Rose took seriously, it was horses.

"Anyway," Katherine concluded, "just think about it. We could totally carpool, and it means more horse time for you. It's just one week, Monday through Friday."

"Think about?" Shelby grinned. "I'm going to obsess about it!"

Dr. Simone returned about then with a plate of fresh, warm sugar cookies, so the girls were distracted for a few moments. Katherine and Dr. Simone resumed their conversation about Swann Johnson, while Rose and Shelby looked through Shelby's massive collection of horse books.

"You are a library, Shelby," Rose said in amazement. "And you've actually read all of these?"

Shelby had, in fact, pretty much memorized most of them, but she didn't want to seem weird. She had learned from her years at Metro School for Girls in the city that *horse girls* were considered over-the-top. Still, she nodded. "They're mostly pictures and instructional stuff, though," she said to hide her embarrassment.

Rose pursed her lips. "If I had read all of these books, I'd announce it to everyone I met. 'Hi, I'm Shelby Simone, and I am a walking equine encyclopedia!'" She gave a sassy snap that Shelby would never actually do in real life, and Shelby laughed.

"You can borrow them sometime if you like. I mean, not all of them at once, but if you want to read any of them, you can." Shelby gestured invitingly at the bookshelves.

Rose selected a few books to borrow with a promise to get them back to Shelby before their next riding lesson. She mostly wanted to look at the giant glossy pictures of perfect-looking horses, but as she explained to Shelby with a shrug, there were probably some interesting facts in there, too.

All too soon, Katherine's brother Drew–who served as the girls' official chauffeur–arrived, and Rose hopped into the backseat, thanking Shelby again for letting her borrow the books. Before Katherine joined her, she said, "Remember, Shelby," and pointed at her head mysteriously.

"Does that mean something?" Shelby's mom asked her as Drew and the girls drove away.

"Kind of," Shelby said. She needed to think about this before she talked to her parents about it, but horse camp was awfully tempting. But if it was going to happen, she needed to work fast.

Shelby's Diary

Diary, if there is one thing I have learned about the horse world so far, it is that things are always going on.

Tonight, in between chatting with my mother about Stupid Swann Johnson and playing Uno, Katherine found out that she's going to be a junior counselor at horse camp. I didn't even know horse camp was a thing! Of course, I wouldn't know about it, since it happened before I showed up. I probably could have looked it up on the internet, I guess. I mean, I knew horse camp was a thing, but it was over! Ugh. I feel kind of silly, Diary.

But anyway, the point is that they're having another session, and Katherine is going to be there every day, so I would have a ride there with Drew and Katherine, right? Katherine is going to be the junior counselor for the Green group, and I would be the Junior group, so we could hang out on breaks and stuff.

The problem is, I don't know how to ask Mom and Dad about it. They're just not into this horse thing. I can tell that they're happy that I'm out doing stuff, and they LOVE Katherine and Rose, so I can tell that they're really proud or whatever. They're happy that I'm happy. But I can also tell that they weren't really planning on this being a long-term thing. The other day I was talking about where I might store my saddle once I'm advanced enough to start getting my own equipment, and Dad started in with that "Whoa there, Sport" stuff that made me feel like... idk like they aren't actually planning on me continuing riding after the two-month deal is up?

I know I should just suck it up and ask, and that they won't be mad at me for just asking about it, but I hate feeling dumb in front of my parents. They're so smart, and sometimes my thoughts go faster than my logic, and I feel like I make a fool of myself when they point out the obvious problems with my plans.

Logically, I think it makes sense. I'll be making friends and active and learning stuff during the day while Mom and Dad are at the site. They'll probably be an easy sell. It's just asking them to buy me stuff when they already don't love horses. At least, not the way I do. And I get the sneaking suspicion they wish I'd find another hobby. Amy's dad—back in the city—used to buy her stuff he hated all the time, just because he wanted her to like him. I don't want my parents to think I'm just spending all of their money.

Then again, it is educational, and they love education. I love education. I love horses. This makes sense, right, Diary? Or am I just being reactive, as my dear old dad would say?

Mom would say I should sleep on it, but it's really kind of hard to sleep when you can't stop thinking about the sales pitch you're going to use for horse camp. Why waste rehearsal time?

Diary, it's times like this that I wish I had school and homework to keep my brain busy.

Don't you dare tell anyone I said that!

Chapter Two

The Great Camp Debate

"Paging Miss Shelby Simone. Miss Simone, your party is waiting for you in the main arena. Please meet your party in the main arena. Paging Miss Simone!"

Bill had his hands cupped around his mouth like a megaphone as he made his announcement.

Shelby kind of heard what he said, but first, she noticed what felt like millions of eyes on her. She shook her shoulders and blinked. Bill, Katherine, and Rose were staring at her. Katherine even looked a little alarmed. Had she really just zoned out in her riding lesson?

She sure had. Coins had obediently taken her to the far end of the arena, but instead of zig-zagging through a series of cones as a steering exercise, they were standing next to the far gate that led to another aisleway. Coins was a very well-trained lesson horse, so when Shelby stopped steering him, he had very kindly slowed to a halt.

Shelby immediately flushed a dark red. *Paying attention to where you're going is the number one fundamentally necessary uber-super important rule of riding, Shelby!* she practically yelled at herself. Thank goodness Coins hadn't decided to take advantage of her mental absence and pull some sort of trick. They could've galloped across half the county by now.

Taking a moment to gather her reins and her wits, Shelby asked Coins to walk forward. This time, she turned him in a wide circle to the left. She approached the line of cones again, this time head-on. She gently pulled her right elbow back and tried to feel long in her right leg. She shifted her weight to her right seat bone and let her leg feel like it was stretching all the way from her hip to the ground. Coins headed to the right, curving around the first cone. She then pulled her left elbow back and shifted to her left seat bone, stretching her left leg long. Coins curled around the next cone.

The tricky part came at the end of the line, where Bill had placed the cones closer together. That meant she had to pay close attention to her timing in giving Coins his cues to turn. By moving her elbow and increasing pressure on one side, she was asking him to turn. To make matters complicated, though, when she pulled on the reins, the Appaloosa wanted to stop. So, on top of telling him where to go, she had to also remind him to keep walking forward. *"Keep your hips loose, don't clench up, and tap him with your heels when he starts to slow down,"* Bill had told her.

It was a lot to remember at once. During her first lesson, Bill described horseback riding as the only sport where you simultaneously use every muscle in your body while trying to do the least possible work. At the time, Shelby hadn't really appreciated what that meant. Now, she realized that riding was possibly the most physically challenging activity she had ever tried in her life.

The first few lessons had been fine since Bill hadn't let her off the lunge line—a long rope attached to Coins' bridle with a series of clips. Bill controlled the horse using the lunge line to steer him and stop him and made different gestures with a long whip to ask him to walk forward, or eventually, when Shelby was ready, to trot.

Then Bill unclipped the lunge line one day and said, "Why don't you give us a lap of the arena, Shelby? Go do a round of the whole thing." Bill had smiled widely, and just for a moment, Shelby felt like she could float right up from the saddle.

Unfortunately, that feeling only lasted a little while. After a few hesitant steps, Shelby got a little off-balance, and Coins calmly stopped while she regained her seat.

Shelby had felt like that first trip around the arena took about an hour. She and Coins would walk a few steps, Shelby would make a mistake, and Coins would stop. Then she would kick him timidly, which he ignored. A little harder kick, and he might shift his weight. An even harder kick, and he'd decide she really meant it. Over and over again.

But that was a few weeks ago. Today, she had mounted up and immediately walked Coins in a full loop around the arena by herself. In fact, Bill only attached the lunge line when they were working on trotting, which was—in Shelby's opinion—a somewhat scary and maybe unnecessary faster gait than the walk.

That meant they spent a lot of time working on steering exercises like this one, which was supposed to make Shelby think about when and how she gave Coins steering cues. It looked so easy, but Shelby found herself physically and mentally tired at the end of the row of cones. She looked back after halting her horse. They'd knocked over three cones. Not bad—last time it had been five.

"Did that seem hard?" Bill asked, peering up at Shelby. "How did that feel overall?"

Shelby frowned. "I'm still overthinking it, but I thought less that time."

"You did! I don't know where you went right before you started the course, but it helped. You were actually breathing and riding for the last few cones. It was just those three you creamed." He pointed at the cones.

It was true. Shelby and Coins had sailed through the first two cones, then something went to pieces because Coins had knocked over the next three cones with his feet. He'd even stepped on the last one, leaving it a pathetic, crumpled shape on the sawdust.

"But then here, in the end," Bill continued, walking up the cones, "This is where I didn't even measure where I put them, and you nailed it here. So, tell me about it. How'd that trip go?"

Bill was a fan of asking his riders what they had felt or noticed when they were riding, so they could figure out what kind of challenge they might be facing. Sometimes riders got tense in a certain way that could keep their horse from feeling like it can do what's being asked, Bill explained.

"You might be kicking with all your might, but if your hands are saying stop, your horse is probably going to prefer to stop than to waste all that effort moving faster. The only way your horse is going forward is if your hands, your seat, your legs, and your brain all say that it's a good idea."

"Well," Shelby started, biting her lower lip. "I am super distracted. And then I got embarrassed when I realized that I had zoned out. I'm sorry about that, by the way. I know I should never do that." Bill nodded patiently and Shelby continued. "So, then I got us in a really good position to start the course, but then after the second cone, I thought I was too far to the inside, so I asked Coins to turn too soon. I thought we didn't have enough room. Then I tried to get him straight again so I could correct it, but I asked too hard, and we turned the other way." Shelby visualized the ride in her mind, remembering each cone in the pattern.

"How do you remember all that?" Rose exclaimed from the bleachers. Katherine shushed her, but Bill just laughed.

"Some riders do that," he explained. "I can tell you about every turn in a barrel run, but I can't tell you how I warmed up, or what I ate for dinner that day. Others go into performance autopilot mode and don't remember a course five seconds after they're done. Neither is better, and both tend to win a lot. Lots of sports psychology stuff out there if you girls want to read up on it." Bill winked at Shelby. He knew Shelby would want to know all about it, but research outside of school wasn't really Rose's sort of thing.

"So," Bill continued, "I have to ask this, but is everything okay? Is there anything you need to talk to an adult about? You're not normally distracted away from horses, so I just have to ask. As your sports coach and riding teacher and all that stuff."

"Oh yeah." Shelby blushed again. "Everything is fine. I just heard about horse camp."

"Ah." Bill nodded knowingly. "So, you're wondering if you should try it out and wish that I could somehow speak to your parents about it for you so you don't have to have any awkward conversations with your parents?"

How does he know all this? Shelby thought. Her face must have shown her shock, too, because Bill burst out laughing.

"Shelby, look around. Something like 50% of the students here are girls in your age group. A smart businessman knows his customers. I'd say I'm almost as familiar with the mind of a brand-new horse person as I am with the mind of a horse. Especially," he took care to say this part with extra kindness, "those who don't exactly come from horsey backgrounds."

Shelby blushed even deeper. She had been hoping Bill just hadn't noticed that her parents hadn't been at the barn for several weeks.

"You might be wondering if you're good enough for horse camp," Bill continued, waggling his fingers in air quotes. "And Shelby, the thing is, none of us are good enough when it comes to riding horses. But we all keep trying, because we love it, and we know that we have the ability to learn more."

Shelby let his words settle in.

"And we all gotta start somewhere," he added. "So yes, new students are absolutely welcome at horse camp. I'm not gonna ask your parents for you, but if you want me to be there to answer any questions when you ask them, I'd be happy to help. Now." He patted Coins on the shoulder. "Go walk this beast around one lap in each direction and you can be done. You worked hard today."

After her lesson, Shelby untacked Coins carefully, first removing the bridle and replacing it with a halter. It had taken her a bit to understand the difference between the two—the bridle had a bit and reins attached for steering, while a halter just had straps that wrapped around the horse's face. Rings on the halter gave riders a place to clip lead ropes or lunge ropes to guide their horse. Now that she'd learned the difference, she easily clipped two long chains known as cross ties to Coins' halter. This kept him standing still in the aisleway while she removed his saddle next.

When she was done untacking Coins, she gave him a brushing with his favorite body brush, being sure to give him some extra scratches on his favorite spot on his neck. "You were a good buddy today," she said to Coins. "You could've dumped me and run to freedom, but you didn't. Thanks, Coins." She gave him a few extra treats after she put him back in his stall.

Rose came around the corner first. She and Katherine had been saddling their horses for their lesson, which was immediately after Shelby's. That way, the three could carpool together, and cheer each other on from the view room or the bleachers that overlooked the arena.

Of course, Shelby thought with dismay, *they get to ride every day since they have their own horses.*

"Where did you go?" Rose asked with a mix of curious and genuine concern on her face.

"I had to untack Coins," Shelby replied. "You know that."

"No, silly," Rose rolled her eyes. "When you were daydreaming out there. Where did you go?"

"Oh, that. I was just trying to figure out how I could pitch the idea of horse camp to my parents. Tomorrow is the last day to sign up, you know," Shelby admitted. She could hear the disappointment in her voice.

"You still haven't asked them yet?" Katherine exclaimed.

"We riding today, girls?" Bill's voice boomed from the arena. He could clearly see the three of them chatting just outside the arena gate.

Rose and Katherine led their horses into the arena, and Shelby settled herself on the bleachers beside the ring, where Rose and Katherine had sat earlier for her lesson.

For the next hour, Shelby was barely aware of the lesson playing out in front of her. Bill was asking the two more experienced girls to trot their horses through the cones, only Rose hadn't quite gotten the pace for the last few cones in the pattern. Since they were at different distances than the others, she either turned Whisper too quickly or not quickly enough. Many cones were stepped on as she tried to get the hang of it.

Katherine and Comet weren't having too bad of a time, but the Quarter Horse mare really didn't see the point in trotting through the cones. She wanted to walk the pattern instead, so Katherine had to use a lot of leg aids, keeping her moving forward with gentle movements of her thighs and calves.

"Think about your arms, Katherine," Shelby heard Bill say patiently. "Are they letting her move forward, or are you tense somewhere?"

Eventually, Shelby stopped paying attention at all. She had to arrange her horse camp strategy.

Later that night, Shelby surprised her parents at the dinner table.

"Mom? Dad? I kind of have something I want to talk to you about after dinner." She spoke quietly and nervously.

Dr. Simone put down her fork. "What's wrong, Shelby?" She frowned with concern.

"Nothing," Shelby said quickly. That was exactly what she didn't want her parents to think. "I just have an idea that I want to share with you."

"Ooh, I like ideas," exclaimed Shelby's dad. "What kind of proposal are you percolating, Sport?"

"Well, it's about the rest of this summer," Shelby said. "But I don't want to get into it without my notes."

"Notes?" questioned Mr. Simone.

Shelby grinned, "You always said presentation is 50% of communication, Dad. So, I've been working on my presentation deck."

Shelby's dad beamed. "I can't wait for the day you defend your doctorate, Shelby. But in the meantime, I'll be glad to observe your presentation." And with that, the family enjoyed the rest of their dinner over chatter about pottery samples from the dig site.

After dinner, the family gathered in the den. Shelby handed her parents each a flyer. She'd asked Bill for some written information about horse camp, and he had been happy to provide her with a sheet of paper that outlined the dates, cost, and requirements for the impromptu second round of horse camp. "Since we've never done a second run before, it's a little less expensive and a little less formal," Bill had said with a wink. "I think you'd like it, Shelby, but make sure your folks are on board."

Shelby felt a little queasy inside as she started to speak. "Thank you for joining me here tonight," she said to her parents. It seemed a little formal, but that's how her parents had always started their speeches when they were presenting at schools or conventions.

"As you know, Old Quarry Lake School is currently closed due to renovations and an archaeological dig."

"Yes, I believe I may have heard of that," Shelby's father jokingly interrupted. After all, he was half of the team leading the dig. Shelby's mom elbowed him, and he stopped laughing. "I'm sorry. Please continue, Miss."

Shelby didn't let the interruption make her nervous. In fact, it kind of made her feel a little less serious. "Thank you, Dad. In consideration of this fact, I understand that there may be extra summer this year, which means you guys will be gone longer, and I may start school late.

"To keep me occupied, I suggest sending me to the new surprise week of horse camp," she continued, picking up speed and confidence. "As you can see from the flyer I have handed out, it's not super expensive. In fact, I am willing to donate my past two allowances and my next two allowances to cover the cost. I don't need any extra equipment, and Drew is willing to drive. Plus, I get to spend the summer learning things and hanging out with my friends and being active and not just sitting around feeling sad about leaving the city, and it would be really cool if I went," she blurted out in a fast rush of words. Her nerves had gotten the best of her, after all.

Shelby's parents were silent. They looked at the paper, then looked at Shelby. Shelby felt a little dizzy and nervous, but this was it. There was no turning back now.

"Honey, that sounds great," Shelby's mom finally broke the silence. "Actually, they know for a fact that school's starting late this year. We've got to get a durable enclosure set up for the site before we can let people into the area again. Plus, the school needs to set up portable classrooms that will be used until they can get construction running again. Who knew that building a school would be such a nightmare for them?" She paused. "Amazing for us, though. We're just starting to lift the cover on an entirely new civilization."

"We were going to ask if you wanted to do something like this, Sport," Shelby's dad picked up where her mom left off. "There's not really a community center where you could take classes like you did in the city, but we were thinking you could get into some kind of online class. Sending you to the barn sounds like the best plan for all of us."

"We'll have to coordinate with Katherine's parents, though," Shelby's mom mentioned. "We need to make sure Drew is really okay with this, though I suspect he is." Drew was handsomely rewarded for transporting his sister and her friends to and from the barn, as his gigantic homemade computer demonstrated.

Shelby was in disbelief. "You're not mad that I want to spend more time with horses?"

"Of course not, Sport." Shelby's dad chuckled. "I have no idea why you want to do that, but it seems to be your thing. Even if it smells bad, is completely terrifying, and everything costs way too much."

It was Shelby's turn to interrupt, "I'll give up my allowance," she said hurriedly.

"No need for that, Sport," Shelby's dad said. "Maybe down the road, we can talk about how you're going to pay for all of your stinky horse stuff, but this summer is kind of a special case. We can definitely afford horse camp, especially if it gets you and your stinky horse stuff out of the house and enjoying the summer!"

Shelby smiled from ear to ear. She couldn't believe how easy that had been. All that worrying, and for nothing. She was going to horse camp!

Shelby's Diary

Horse camp is ON, Diary!

I don't know why I was so worried. My parents are the best. Sure, they moved me across the state from all of my friends and the world I once knew—just like Swann Johnson, actually. But they really have come through with the horse stuff. LOL

My presentation was rough, Diary. I knew what I wanted to say, but then when I was standing up there talking to them, I felt so silly. Like everything I said wasn't important.

But then when I started thinking about it, it made a lot of sense. I was just asking if I could go to horse camp. Yes, it would have made me sad if they'd said no, but I don't think it would've been a big deal. You know what I mean?

Actually, I don't really think they would've said no, even if I didn't have an extra summer and nothing to do.

Mom called Bill tonight and got me enrolled. She's going to need to sign some more paperwork, but we can do that at my next lesson. Then I get a whole week of uninterrupted pony time!

On the first day, the kids who are coming to camp for the first time have to do what Bill calls Placement Testing. That means we do a little paper quiz, and we also get to ride to show what we know. Rose and Katherine say I'll definitely ace the quiz, but I'm kind of nervous about the riding part. Especially after I zoned out on Coins the other day! So embarrassing!

I think I'll do a quick run-through of Encyclopedia of the Horse to see if there's anything I'm forgetting, and then maybe go through a couple of back issues of

Young Rider magazine. But I don't think I really need to study too much for this quiz. Ooh, I do need to study leg anatomy, Diary. I keep calling the pastern the fetlock, and the fetlock the pastern.

Wish me luck, Diary. This is going to be the horse-iest summer ever, of all time! WOO HOO!

Chapter Three

Placement Testing

"You've got this," Shelby said matter-of-factly. She had said the same phrase to herself over and over again as she got ready for her horse camp placement testing session. She had smoothed and patted every possible wrinkle on her one pair of riding tights. She had cleaned and conditioned her paddock boots. She had even squirted a bit of her mom's least expensive perfume on the inside brim of her riding helmet. Her father said that the smell of Shelby's riding equipment was *sheer olfactory mayhem and devastation*, so Shelby kept her horse gear in a paper bag in the garage. Since she had cleaned them up so nicely, she had been permitted to keep everything in her room as she got ready for horse camp placement testing. This was a big day, after all.

Shelby had read and re-read the placement testing manual Bill had given her once her parents had completed the registration process. The placement testing took place outside of a regular riding lesson. Since this was a last-minute addition to the summer schedule, students were scheduled based on availability, not skill level, which Shelby thought was pretty chaotic. She might be riding with some really good riders today, but she also might be riding with little, tiny kids who couldn't steer, too.

You've got this. You've got this! YOU'VE GOT THIS! Shelby thought to herself again and again.

And yet when her mother appeared in the corner of the mirror to announce her ride to the barn had arrived, Shelby jumped and yelped in surprise. "Mom! You can't sneak up on me like that."

Shelby's mom chuckled warmly. "You're in the zone. But you're right. You've got this, Shelby!"

Shelby blushed. Had she been chanting the phrase out loud? Thankfully, her mother was already heading downstairs, so Shelby grabbed her helmet and followed her.

At the door, Dr. Simone handed her daughter a bag with a small snack and a bottle of water in it and waved at Drew and Katherine waiting in the driveway. She was heading back to the dig site, so she got in her car as Shelby joined Katherine in the backseat of Drew's Honda. "Remember," she shouted through the car window. "You've got this, sweetie. I'll see you afterward for a celebratory pizza dinner."

"Your mom is so sweet," Katherine said as Shelby buckled up. "I want to do a celebratory pizza dinner tonight."

Shelby grinned, "It's actually a kind of code. My mom doesn't really like eating at restaurants a lot, so when we get pizza, it's kind of a special occasion on its own. We celebrate eating pizza every time we eat pizza." The girls chuckled, and Shelby continued. "They're going to be at the dig until at least seven tonight, so there's no way we're cooking dinner. They're bringing pizza home, instead."

Drew looked in the rearview mirror. "Hey, did you grow up in the same house we did? I actually believed sausage pizza was a bad thing until I was six."

Katherine rolled her eyes. "I think you've made up for it by now. Didn't you eat an entire sausage pizza the last time we went to Pasquale's?"

"Yes, ma'am I did!" Drew exclaimed proudly. "I'm a growing boy, Katherine." He turned his gaze to Shelby in the rearview mirror. "So, what's your favorite pizza topping?"

Shelby blushed. "You're going to make fun of me. Everyone does," she exclaimed as Drew and Katherine started to protest. She took a deep breath and said:

"I love pineapple and onion. It's the best. It's my favorite."

There was a moment of shocked silence in the vehicle. Finally, Drew spoke. "Shelby, that is absolutely... *metal*." He nodded his approval. "It takes a strong woman to know what she likes, even if it makes her breath smell like armpits and breaks every American food rule."

Katherine nodded. "Sweet and savory are actually great together. There are a lot of tropical influences in some of the recipes my mother got from her family in China. I like sweet and spicy best. Have you tried pineapple and banana pepper?"

It was Shelby's turn to look shocked. "That sounds amazing," she said, her mouth watering.

As they continued toward Old Quarry Lake Farms, Drew, Katherine, and Shelby cheerfully chatted about uncommon food combinations they loved. Shelby completely forgot to be nervous about her placement test until they pulled into the barn driveway. But her nerves came right back at the sound of gravel under the Honda's wheels.

Still, she felt pretty calm as she walked into the barn. Bill had explained the process to her. First, she would meet with the three other people in her test. Then, they would each get to groom and tack up their usual lesson horses. The other counselors and junior counselors—including Katherine—would be on hand to help evaluate how well the students did these tasks.

The riding part would happen in the ring. Again, the counselors would help students who weren't ready to steer on their own by leading them or lunging them. Bill would ask the students to do things like walk, trot, halt, steer on their own, and if they were ready canter.

That was where Shelby felt the least confident. Shelby wasn't really cantering yet. Bill had let her try a few strides on the lunge line, but she had felt super disorganized and asked him to stop. She wasn't even trotting off the lunge line very much yet. But that was ok with her, because as Bill was always saying, "We all have to start learning at some point."

After the riding portion, the students would gather in the view room to complete a twenty-question quiz about horses and horsemanship. Shelby wasn't worried about this part at all.

"They're designed to be tricky," Rose had warned Shelby. "You'll want to read them carefully."

Katherine had agreed. "There were some things on there that I didn't know, and I thought I was pretty good at this horse-keeping thing. Bill says there's a method behind his madness, and I guess he's right. Every time I've done camp, I've learned something brand new."

Still, Shelby felt her new friends underestimated the sheer quantity of horse-related material she studied daily. When she had lived in the city, Shelby had always felt a little embarrassed about her obsession. Now that she finally had a way to use her horse knowledge, she felt it was her time to shine.

But Shelby's confidence quickly plummeted when she saw Bill's face. "Shelby, I hate to tell you this, but Coins pulled a shoe this morning."

"Oh no." Shelby was horrified. "Is he ok?" The idea of losing her best equine friend terrified her.

"Of course," Bill said calmly. "It just means that his foot is a little sore right now, so you won't be able to ride him today. The farrier will be out tomorrow to put the horseshoe back on the horse, but in the meantime, Coins will be watching from the sidelines."

Shelby's shoulders slumped. Did that mean she would have to reschedule her placement testing? She'd have to go through those nerves all over again? On the other hand, that might mean more time to study for the written portion…

Shelby's thoughts were interrupted by Bill. As if he could read her mind, he continued, "So I think you'll have your ride Buddy today. Buddy is retired from the show ring, and now he likes to spend his days being lazy and hanging out with kids. I warmed him up for you, so he's ready to go. And good news is you can use the same saddle and bridle you use for Coins. I'm trying not to throw you for too many loops today." Bill winked kindly, but Shelby's stomach felt cold and heavy.

Coins was the only horse she had ever ridden. Ever! Shelby's hands felt clammy. How was she supposed to take a test on a horse she'd never ridden?

Logically, she knew this sort of thing happened all the time. As students progressed through their lessons, they got to ride more and more of the horses living at the barn. But she wasn't even entirely sure she was used to Coins yet, much less ready for a new horse.

Katherine tried to reassure her. "Buddy is a big old sweetheart," she said. "He's super slow. Bill will probably give you a crop to encourage him to move forward."

That made Shelby feel worse. She'd never ridden while holding a riding crop. She'd read about crops, the short whip that some riders used while they rode. Tapping a horse on the shoulder or behind the leg with a crop was supposed to encourage the horse to move forward, especially when tapping with the heels or kicking isn't working.

Shelby felt like steering was hard enough with just two reins to focus on. Adding a crop would just make it harder.

Still, it wasn't like she could drop out of horse camp right here and now. Besides, Coins would be back for camp. Bill and Katherine would be watching, and they both knew how Shelby could ride in her regular lessons, so it wouldn't be a big deal. *Right?* Shelby asked herself. *No big deal! This is no problem!*

Shelby almost felt better about the situation, but then she turned around and saw Buddy. Buddy was enormous. While Coins stood a majestic 15 hands—or 60 inches—tall at the base of his neck, Buddy had to be at least 20 hands tall. Shelby stared up at his face and felt her jaw drop.

"He's not as big as you think," Bill said, noticing the look of fear frozen on Shelby's face. "He's actually just two inches taller than Coins at the withers." Bill touched Buddy at the spot where his neck met his back to demonstrate. "It's just that he has this really long neck, which he insists on wearing upright at all times. Buddy is some kind of draft horse carriage pony cross that we've never figured out." Bill ran his hand along Buddy's neck toward his ears. Even an adult man like Bill could barely reach Buddy's ears.

"So," Bill continued, "we had to ask Buddy to help us with this kind of stuff." He turned to the horse. "Drop it, Buddy," he said, tapping the horse on the neck, right behind his ears.

Without hesitation, Buddy lowered his head to Bill's waist. "It's much easier to brush and get the bridle on down here," he concluded. "But just let me know if you need a hand."

As he walked away, Bill announced that horse camp placement tests officially had begun, but Shelby barely heard him.

She was busy examining Buddy closely. She supposed he had been a palomino horse at some point, but the grey hairs of age and time spent snoozing in the sun had bleached him into the same color as a dirty white rag. As she brushed him, she couldn't tell if she was brushing over mud stains, or just dark patches of hair here and there.

And while Buddy was happy to lower his face to Shelby's level, he couldn't do anything about the rest of his body, which still towered over Shelby's head. *Those two inches make a big difference*, she thought. She tried to reach the stiff-bristled body brush as high up his body as she could, even standing on her tiptoes. All she did was drop the brush. She dropped the brush six times, as a matter of fact. Every time it clanked against the textured concrete aisleway, she blushed deeper and deeper shades of red.

Bill had brought out a small stool so she could hoist the saddle up onto Buddy's back, but she still needed help cinching the girth under the horse's big belly. She just wasn't tall enough to pull the leather straps through the buckles until they were snug.

Luckily for Shelby, Buddy really was the sweetheart Katherine had said. He patiently ignored all of her fumbling and dropping things. He calmly picked up each hoof to be cleaned, even though his feet were the size of Shelby's face, in her estimation.

As she was leading Buddy into the general arena, she thought, *It's a good thing my mom isn't here to watch. She'd be way too scared watching me ride such a big horse. It's not a problem, though. He's just a horse, like Coins.*

Shelby wasn't aware of how wrong she was about Buddy being *just like Coins*, but she was about to find out.

Mounting up was difficult. Instead of using the nice, solid, stable mounting block that was built into the arena wall, she had to use a much taller step stool to get on Buddy. The step stool wobbled as she stepped in the stirrup and jumped into the saddle, so she landed much harder on Buddy's back than she meant to. "I'm so sorry, Buddy. I swear I know better," she whispered as Bill adjusted her stirrups.

"Do you want to warm up on the lunge line?" Bill asked. Shelby looked around. All of the other riders were warming up their horses on a loose rein at the walk, except one little tyke, who looked about four years old. Katherine was leading him around on Petey the saintly pony. She flashed Shelby the thumbs-up signal from across the arena.

Shelby shook her head. "No, I'll just walk him out like everyone else." She didn't want to look like she couldn't at least walk a horse, even if she'd never ridden that horse before.

Besides, she thought to herself, *even my dad figured out how to ride that horse on the trail ride in Kentucky. And he's not even that great at steering a car.*

The thought made her smile, and she wiggled out her shoulders and elbows to relax them before signaling Buddy to walk on with a squeeze of her heels.

Buddy did not walk on. He shifted his weight and sighed.

"You might have to get after him a bit," Bill said. "Give him a big kick. You're interrupting his prime nap time, so tell him to go."

Shelby nudged Buddy even harder with her heels. "Sorry, Buddy," she said again. "I need you to walk."

Buddy refused to move. He chewed on the bit for a moment and sighed again.

This continued for far longer than Shelby could have ever dreamed. Bill would give her instructions, Shelby would do her best to do what Bill asked, and Buddy would do nothing. At one point, he started to take a step forward but thought better of it and put his hoof back on the ground.

Bill shook his head. "This is kind of his thing. Sorry, Shelby. You're doing what you can. Let's start you off on the lunge line so I can step in and convince him to do his job."

Shelby couldn't tell if her face was hot and red because she was embarrassed or because she had just worked very hard to get nowhere. Either way, she knew that her placement test wasn't off to a good start.

Thankfully, everyone seemed to appreciate Buddy's quirks. The other counselors smiled at her and said, *Oh, Buddy* sympathetically as Bill led the pair to the empty end of the arena. With Bill at the other end of the lunge line with a whip to encourage him, Buddy walked and trotted nicely for Shelby.

Then it was time to take the test. Each student was asked to walk half a loop around the arena along the wall. Halfway down the arena wall on each side was the door that led to the barn. Riders would turn at the door and switch directions at the walk. When they got back to the other door, they would trot a circle, canter another circle if they could, and then halt. Bill would meet Shelby there to put her on the lunge line for the trot circle.

The first two students were more experienced, but they still had problems. The first rider's horse was distracted and halted at the end of the arena. She tapped him on the shoulder with a crop, and he moved forward but continued to keep his attention on everything but his rider. Shelby could tell she was getting frustrated, too.

The second rider's horse didn't want to halt. Their canter circle looked more like a hexagon, too, Shelby thought.

Then it was Shelby's turn. "Let's go, Buddy," she said, keeping her elbows and shoulders loose and open while giving him a firm jab with her heels. Buddy surprised her by going exactly as she asked.

As a result, Shelby felt a little jostled in the saddle. She hadn't expected him to walk forward. Plus, Buddy had a pretty big walk, meaning that his natural stride covered far more ground than she was used to with Coins.

Still, Shelby steadied herself and guided Buddy to the wall with her reins and seat. Buddy was picking up speed now. He had a nice, smooth walk, Shelby thought, even if it was a little speedier than she liked.

At the door, Shelby halted Buddy so Bill could clip the lunge line to the rings of the bridle. Shelby loosened her grip on the reins so she wouldn't interfere with Bill's commands to the horse. And the next thing she knew, the world turned upside down for a moment. Buddy moved all of a sudden, and her legs clamped down on the saddle. When everything settled, her heart was pounding, she and Buddy were standing in a different place, and Bill looked angry.

"Wha-what happened?" she stammered. Buddy was snorting and shaking his head.

"Are you alright, Shelby?" Bill asked. His eyebrows were drawn together in a scowl, but he looked more worried than angry now as he looked Shelby over.

"Sure," Shelby said. "But why...?" She wasn't entirely sure what happened, but she was shaking.

"Some fool just slammed the front door of the barn," Bill said grimly. "Buddy spooked. I'm actually impressed you stayed on there. You did great!" A beaming smile broke through his stony expression.

"Buddy spooked?" Shelby was shocked. She had seen videos of spooks before, and they looked very scary. Usually, the horses moved sideways or dashed forward, and the riders almost always got left in the dirt.

Bill nodded. "Yeah. It was a little thing, but more than you needed. I'm sorry, Shelby. I didn't expect someone to slam the door during placement tests. Of all the things a fool could do." Bill trailed off. He seemed to be talking to himself. "But let's do the trot part, and you can be done with your test. Are you good? Think we can do that?"

Shelby nodded, but even as Buddy took his first walk steps, she knew she was lying. Now that she knew what happened, she was suddenly very scared of the way Buddy moved. She felt completely unstable in the saddle, swaying back and forth dramatically as his big back moved her seat bones. She clenched her lower back to stop the movement, and Buddy stopped obediently.

Bill looked back at them. "Everything ok? Was that you or him?"

"We're good," Shelby squeaked back, mostly trying to convince herself. Bill nodded in response. He seemed to know Shelby was bluffing, but he urged Buddy to walk in a circle around him anyway.

After a few strides, Shelby felt herself relax a bit. She'd made it all the way around the ring, so she could do this part, right? She took a few deep breaths to relax and nodded at Bill to ask for the trot.

Buddy lurched forward, and Shelby's entire body jolted. She lost her left stirrup and grabbed desperately at the curved pommel of the saddle in front of her. Buddy instantly halted when she lost her balance, but even though Shelby hadn't fallen off, she was shaking with fear.

Bill was sympathetic. "I wondered if you might not be exactly ready," he said quietly to Shelby. "It's ok, kiddo. It was scary. I was even scared a little for you. Do you want to do a walking loop on the lunge and be done with it, or do you want to try to do the test again after we let the little guy go?" He gestured to the younger child with Petey.

Shelby thought about it. "Let's just be done with it," she decided. Bill nodded, and once she had gathered her stirrup again, he announced that he was going to lunge Buddy for a walk loop, and then Shelby would be finished with the riding portion of her test.

As she took a few deep breaths and tried to shrug off her fear, Shelby could tell that the rest of the counselors were sympathetic. Katherine looked genuinely concerned about her friend, too. She didn't know what the spook had looked like, but she had started on Bill's right side and ended on his left side, facing the other direction. It had clearly been interesting, and that made her stomach churn a little.

Shelby's final walk loop was uneventful. Bill helped her dismount and led Buddy back to the aisle to untack and put the horse back in his stall quickly before Katherine led the last rider through his test.

"Well, I definitely didn't plan on that happening," she muttered as she gave Buddy a piece of the apple her mother had packed for her snack. "Of course, I don't think you planned on it going that way, either." Buddy seemed to sigh in agreement as he chomped on the apple. Juice dripped down his big, wrinkled lips.

All of the students quickly untacked after the tests were concluded and gathered in the view room.

"This is the part I'm going to bomb," whispered the older girl.

"Don't copy off me," said the older boy rider. "I'm just kind of making it up."

Shelby should have felt extra-confident overhearing this, but she didn't. She kept replaying Buddy's spook. She was scared that it happened, excited that she had stayed on, and confused because she couldn't really remember it happening.

Bill was explaining the instructions, but Shelby was barely paying attention. A test was a test, after all, and she had always been exceptionally good at taking tests. She started tuning in just as Bill was saying, "And your time starts now..."

Shelby's Diary

Diary, what is wrong with me? No, seriously. Why can't I pull it together when it comes to horses?

The placement test was humiliating. I've never ridden in front of anyone besides Bill, Katherine and Rose. And my mom, but I doubt she was actually looking at me.

But that wasn't the worst part. I didn't even think about that until we got into the arena. I know how to share an arena with other riders, but I forgot that all of the counselors would be there, too.

And they all saw me, Diary. Every single one of them saw me fail SO HARD!!!!!

Bill says that Buddy used to be a super-fancy show horse. I don't know what type of class he was in. Is there one where horses are judged for standing still and ignoring their rider? I didn't think so, but apparently, I don't know anything about horses. Don't worry, Diary, we'll get to that part. I'm so angry with myself!!

I could NOT get Buddy to walk. I had to get on the lunge line to walk, just like a little baby. Actually, there was a little baby there, Diary, and he didn't go on the lunge. Katherine kept his pony on a lead line, which is much shorter. Still, she says he can walk on his own.

I COULDN'T!!!!!!!!!!!!!!!!!!!!

And then, when I finally did, I was totally worn out from trying. Bill says the hardest thing to do on a horse is not to get tense and tight when things go wrong. I

KNOW THAT NOW, DIARY! My legs are starting to burn. Bill said I would probably be sore, because I don't have to work that hard on Coins, and it's true! I took a bath in Epsom salts as he and my parents recommended, but my hips and outer thighs are pretty uncomfortable.

But let's talk about the highlight of my ride, Diary. Let's talk about the part where Buddy went upside down and backward on me. Some (insert bad name here) slammed a door in the barn, and Buddy freaked out. I don't blame him. I probably would have too, if I had heard it. Instead, my brain was too busy keeping me balanced on the horse as he whirled around in a big spook. I'm glad. Thank you, Brain. I'm glad I don't remember that.

I kind of feel impressed with myself that I stayed on, now that I'm home and on solid ground. I've never ridden anything like that, and I wasn't even jostled. My little reptile brain was working overtime for my survival, as Dad would say.

But then there was my grand finale, Diary. I tried to do the trot loop, and I failed. I super-failed. Buddy trotted, like, two steps, and I lost my stirrup and almost fell off. Just riding a stupid trot. We had JUST trotted, like, ten minutes earlier on the lunge line and I was fine. Buddy has a big trot, but the bounce made it easier to post to—that's where you "rise and fall with the leg on the wall," Diary. Posting trot is where you stand when the horse's outside leg goes forward. I'm terrible at it, but everyone at the barn assures me that it's like riding a bicycle.

But I didn't post, Diary. I got all shaky and scared. Bill was great—he stopped Buddy, and I was fine. I got my stirrup back, did a big walk loop and got off.

BUT I COULDN'T STOP SHAKING AND I'M PRETTY SURE I FAILED THE WRITTEN TEST! AAAAAAAARRRRRRRRGGGG-GGHHHH!

There was a diagram of a leg to label. There were some questions about how much forage a horse needs and what they eat. There was some stuff I know Bill hasn't talked about with me, like when to use different blankets, but I read about that in Horse Keeping for First Timers, *so I think I was okay there. Then a bunch of different breeds—there was a picture of a horse with a description.* "Fancy-Bred in Kentucky. Shows in Saddle Seat and Showmanship. 15 hands high. Gaited." *Stuff like that. My printed test was a little sketchy in the bottom corner, so what I called a Connemara might have been a Welsh Pony.*

Who knows? I was still shaking. I broke my pencil and had to finish the test with a spare pen that someone found in one of the recliner cushions in the view room.

It was miserable, Diary. I won't be shocked if they put me in Pre-Green because of this ridiculous day.

Chapter Four

The Results Are In

Thankfully, Shelby didn't have to wait too long to find out what the adults in charge had thought of her performance during the placement tests.

"Bill texted me already," Shelby's mom said as they ate breakfast the next day. "He said the camp placements will be posted by the time we get there for your lesson this evening."

Shelby paused with her bagel just inches from her mouth. "Tonight?" she squeaked, placing the bagel back on her plate.

Shelby's mom nodded behind her giant mug of strong, dark coffee. "So, I was thinking, if you don't mind getting to your lesson a little early, I could take a break at the site, and we could look together?"

In fact, Shelby didn't mind at all. She loved spending extra time at the barn. She also appreciated that her mom wanted to be there for this big moment. *Ok,* Shelby admitted to herself, *it's not as important as my first steps walking or the first day of school. But it's my first horse camp!*

Plus, Shelby knew that her parents would be busy at the dig site for the first actual day of horse camp. This was almost as good.

Shelby passed the morning nervously dusting her Dresden horses, flipping through her favorite horse books without actually reading them, and wishing either Katherine or Rose would come online to their group chat.

Eventually, it came time for Shelby's lesson. Her mom took a late lunch break as promised and showed up just as Shelby had finished putting on her only pair of breeches, fresh from the wash.

"You know," Shelby's mom said as she got in the car. "If you're going to be at the barn every day, maybe we should buy you a few more pairs of breeches. Maybe a few of those riding sun shirts, too. Want to go to the tack shop tomorrow?"

Shelby burst into a grin. "Are you serious? New breeches?" Shelby had only recently become aware of how expensive horseback riding clothing and equipment could be.

Her mom grinned in the rearview mirror. "I'm not doing the wash every night. Besides, they can't go in the dryer, which means you'd be wearing squelching britches every day."

Shelby laughed at the mental image, then cringed as she thought about the potential for chafing. "Thanks, Mom. I can use my allowance to pay for it."

Her mother brushed her off with a wave of the hand. "These are strange times, Shelby. Just remember this when your father and I are old and grey and need you to take care of us."

Shelby didn't want to think that far into the future, so she didn't. Instead, she thought ahead to her lesson tonight. Coins should be back in shape, and she'd be able to redeem herself for her sloppy trot during the placement test.

She was so focused that it almost slipped her mind why her mother was there in the first place. When Dr. Simone pulled into a parking spot instead of dropping Shelby off at the front door, it came back to her with a jolt. *Horse camp placements!*

While she hadn't asked her mom where the placements were posted, it didn't take a lot of searching to find them. There were three crisp, new pieces of white paper posted on the bulletin board outside of the view room. Everything that had been posted for more than a few hours was covered in dust, so these had just been pinned there.

Shelby gulped and walked up to the list labeled Junior. She scanned the list quickly, twice, but didn't see her name. She gulped. Had Bill forgotten that she had signed up? Had her parents forgotten to pay their deposit? She took a deep breath and read the list slowly. Surely, she had just scanned over her own name.

But it wasn't there. Shelby read the list again and again, but her name simply wasn't on the Junior list.

Her heart fluttered in her chest, and her face felt cold and pale. She quickly scanned the other lists to see if she'd mistakenly been added to another list.

There it was, plainly written:

Rider: Shelby Simone
Horse: Coins

Only somehow, for some reason, it was on the list labeled Green.

Shelby wrinkled her nose in confusion. But that was for kids. There were six-year-olds in the Green group.

Suddenly, Shelby had a lot to think about. She wasn't going to make new friends. Instead, she was going to spend the summer with little kids who couldn't ride, learning about basic horse stuff she already knew with kids who probably couldn't even spell stifle, much less point to the correct joint of the horse.

And then she realized the very worst thing of all. *Katherine is a Junior Counselor for the Green group! Katherine would be teaching her!* Shelby suddenly felt like she needed to cry.

Her mother, on the other hand, was thrilled. "Green! Well, that's really, um, verdant, Shelby!"

Shelby couldn't respond. She was absolutely stunned by the fact that she was going to be in her friend's baby group for camp, and her mother was trying to tell her that green was green.

Shelby had stepped away from the bulletin board, and her mother had somehow coaxed her into the view room. Shelby's body felt numb, but the thoughts were racing through her head.

Her feelings changed rapidly. She was mad about failing the placement test. Obviously, she had done far worse than she had expected to be put in the baby group. She was sad that she hadn't done well. She desperately wanted another chance. And she was really nervous about how she would break the news to Katherine. How could Katherine be friends with a baby rider from the baby rider group?

Shelby noticed that her mother was looking at her with a concerned look on her face. That brought her back to reality. She took a deep breath in and let it out slowly.

"I can tell something's wrong," her mom said. "But I have no idea what it is. Can you tell me, sweetie?"

Shelby shook her head no. She knew that if she started to speak, all of the things she was feeling would come out in a disorganized mess. She felt hot tears forming in her eyes and begged herself to calm down. *Don't cry, don't cry, don't cry!* she chanted to herself.

But it was too late. Shelby's shoulders shook as she gulped in a big sob of air.

Just then, she heard the view room door open. Blindly, Shelby dashed to the bathroom and shut the door behind her quickly.

Since a lot of riders came directly from work or school, the bathroom served as a private changing area. In addition to being bigger than most single bathrooms, it had a few shelves and hooks for folks who brought an extra change of clothes. Best of all, there was a large round stool in the corner where Shelby could hide until she didn't feel like crying anymore. *Or until the end of the world,* Shelby added to herself. *That wouldn't be bad, either.*

On the other side of the door, Shelby could hear her mother speaking to someone else. The door muffled most of the sound, but Shelby's mom was clearly standing very close to the bathroom door.

"I'm not sure what happened," her mom was saying. "We were looking at the lists, and she turned very pale, so I brought her in here. I thought she was going to cry, but then she ran into the toilet. I wonder if she might have eaten something that didn't agree with her?"

Way to go, Mom, Shelby wailed in her mind. *Now everyone is going to think I'm some crybaby with poopie pants!*

"Sure thing," she heard her mom say next. "I'm going to check on her, and we'll come find you. That's OK—if she's not all right, we'll just go home."

What did it all mean? Shelby wondered. *Who is Mom talking to?*

In the silence, Shelby realized her urge to cry had passed. Her breathing had returned to normal. *The worst possible thing happened, and the world did not end,* she reassured herself.

She ran cold water into the sink and splashed her face with it, trying hard not to splash the walls or her shirt. She dried her hands and face off with a paper towel and opened the door to the bathroom just as her mom was about to knock on it.

"Shelby, sweetie. You scared me!" Her mom gathered her into her arms for a big hug. Shelby let her. A hug from her mom felt really good after finding out she was a baby Green rider.

After a few warm moments, Shelby explained. "I'm sorry, Mom. I'm fine, really. I was just shocked that I'm in the Green group." She steadied herself with a big deep breath. "That group is for *children*. Like six-year-olds." Thinking about it made her want to cry again, so she dove back into her mom's big hug.

Shelby's mother patted her daughter's hair, which wasn't quite controlled with a ponytail and a headband. "I expect that's why Bill just came in here looking for you," she replied. "He seemed to think you'd want to talk to him."

Shelby's tummy did another dance. Had Bill put her in the wrong group and come to apologize and fix it? "Did he say where he was going?" she asked her mom urgently.

"Sweetie, I think you need to sit here for a second and drink a juice box and calm down. You are awfully pale." Shelby's mom patted her face, checking for heat or clamminess.

Sitting down and drinking a juice box sounded very good to Shelby, so she sat down at the dining table in the view room. Her mother handed her the small lunch bag that she used to pack Shelby's barn snack. Inside, Shelby found her water bottle, a juice box, and a handful of baby carrots. Baby carrots just happened to be a favorite of both Shelby and Coins. She couldn't wait to share those with him later.

"Drink your juice, Shelby," her mom said. "I'll go grab Bill. Be right back, Sweetie!"

Obediently, Shelby took deep breaths and drank her juice while flipping through a *Practical Horseman* magazine someone had left on the table. She was midway through an article about hip stability over cross-country jumping courses and thinking about how scary that sounded when her mother returned with Bill.

"Hey Shelby," he said with a customary tip of his cowboy hat. Bill was probably the only person in Old Quarry Lake who wore a cowboy hat, but as a world champion barrel racer, Shelby supposed he had earned the right.

He made his way to the table where Shelby was sitting and took a seat across from her. She closed the magazine and sat up straighter. She felt a blush creeping across her face. This didn't look like an apology. It looked like a lecture!

"I imagine you're a little confused about the whole Green thing," he started. He smiled sympathetically. "I want you to know it wasn't easy to figure out where to put you. Shelby, in all my however many years of running this camp, you are the only student who has ever gotten a perfect score on the written test."

"What?" Shelby yelped. She had been convinced she'd bombed the test after that terrible, terrible ride on Buddy. She'd been shaking and couldn't think straight. She shook her head.

Bill's smile was enormous. "You got 'em all! I particularly liked how you answered the Name the Breed questions with an essay about which horses they *could* be based on the description. I suppose Franklin the grey pony could be a Welsh Pony or a Connemara. I'd always reckoned Fancy was obviously a Saddlebred, but you came up with some good reasons why she could be a Kentucky Mountain Saddle horse or Standardbred."

Shelby blushed, but Bill continued.

"When it comes to the actual book-learning part of this camp, you could probably teach all of us a thing or two, Shelby. I mean that." He nodded at Shelby's wide-eyed look of disbelief. "You really know your stuff. But here's the thing—you're brand new at riding.

"Now, I don't want you to think you're bad at riding. Quite the opposite, given how you stuck that spook Buddy threw at you. You've got a knack for this riding thing, but you've really just started. That put me in a tough spot. Is it worse for me to let you get bored in the lessons part or do I put you in the part where you'll learn more, but the riding is a whole lot tougher."

He paused and folded his hands over each other. "So, I decided to put you in a group where you don't have to feel overwhelmed in the riding part. There's going to be a lot of riding in this camp, and I don't want you to be overwhelmed.

I felt like that would be more frustrating to you than having to sit through a basic horse anatomy lesson."

He stopped there and Shelby thought about what he said. He was right. The riders in the Junior group were going to want to do things Shelby wasn't ready to do on a horse, like a canter and trot over poles on the ground. On the other hand, riding with the Green kids would give her the chance to work on her posting trot and steering.

"Here's a little thought," Bill said. "How about I send you home with the Junior kids' workbook, so you can get a peek at their lessons to keep you busy? Obviously, you know it all, already, though," he said with a warm chuckle and a wink.

Shelby smiled back. What Bill said made sense, and she was glad he had taken the time to explain it to her.

"Thanks, Bill," she said. "I guess I was a little surprised to see my name in the…" She swallowed before she said it out loud, "Green group." It felt a little weird to say, but it didn't feel so shameful now. "But it makes sense. What you said about the riding part," she clarified. Now that she considered it, the idea of bobbing along, trying to get her balance to post a trot while other kids cantered fast laps and jumped fences around her, was actually pretty scary.

"So, I'll see you first thing Monday morning for horse camp. Bright and early." He looked like he was about to issue a warning but stopped himself. "That's right—you always come out here with the Wilsons. I don't need to worry. They're early for everything. In fact," he said, peering out the view room door. "Katherine's here already, and her lesson isn't even for another two hours. Anyway, when you're done here, Coins is good to go for your lesson this week. I've got his stuff out for him."

Shelby paled. *Katherine is here!* That meant that Katherine already knew about Shelby's camp placement, too.

As Bill left the view room, Shelby's mom finally piped up. "I am so proud of you, Shelby," she started. "A perfect score on the test. That's awesome!" She put up her hand for a fist bump. Shelby had to smile as her knuckles bumped her mom's. That really was something to be proud of.

Furthermore, Bill had complimented her riding. What was it he said? "You've got a knack for this riding thing?" Suddenly, Shelby felt pretty good, after all the events of the past few minutes.

She followed her mother out of the view room after taking a quick peek in the bathroom mirror to attempt to coax her hair back into a ponytail. As she heard the door click behind her, she looked up, coming face to face with Katherine and Rose. And then she remembered. *Green group!*

Shelby's Diary

Everything is so weird and confusing and I cry like a baby. Diary, is this just normal growing-up stuff, or is this horse stuff that's making the growing-up stuff feel worse?

You will never believe the day I had, Diary. I'm in the Green group.

Not only did I not expect anything other than the Junior group, but I didn't expect to have so many feelings about it. I almost cried about it!!!!!! Cried about going to horse camp. I didn't have horse camp to cry about last summer!

I'm going to be in the baby group. The riders in there are going to be so much younger than I am. Okay, like two years younger, but two years is a lot. Especially when they're just little kids.

And speaking of being a kid, there I was, sipping on a juice box looking all pathetic when Bill came in to tell me I aced the written test part. No wonder he put me in the baby group if I'm going to cry every time I don't get my way.

But my feelings were really hurt. I guess I got my mind set on being in the Junior group. I thought that being in the younger kids' group meant I wasn't good enough. And from what Bill said, that's kind of true, but only right now. In fact, he really complimented the way I rode Coins tonight. I managed to post an entire lap of the arena by myself, Diary! No lunge line! Me steering and posting at the same time! IT WAS SO COOL AND NOTHING BAD HAPPENED!!!!! YAHOOOO!!!!

Talking to Katherine about it was really weird, though. She's basically going to be teaching me. She said it wasn't going to be as weird as I thought, but things still felt off. Maybe it was me. It's been a big day, like I said. I guess we're going to be spending the entire day together, though. Amy Jackie and I used to do that at the Community Center courses we took during the summer, so I think that part will be okay. Just... thinking of your bestie as your teacher is weird, isn't it?

Tomorrow we're taking a Simone Family Field Trip to what Dad calls "The Nearest Semblance of Civilization". It's an hour away in the opposite direction from the city. I suppose it actually is a city, but a much smaller one than home.

Mom and Dad have a meeting with some professors at the university about the dig there, so after that, we'll head to HorsePro Tack Emporium. They have EVERYTHING horse! I've been lurking on their online catalog for years. I even have a wish list, but don't tell anyone about that. LOL

I'm so excited to go to a new mega-huge tack store, Diary. I don't even care if that sounds nerdy. I'm a horse person! It's what we do!

Chapter Five

The Opposite of Shopping

Sitting in the backseat for an hour and a half while their car zipped deeper and deeper into the Appalachian hills had been tolerable. The views were stunning. As the road wound higher and higher, Shelby watched as the thick fog turned the peaks of the hills below them into dark islands floating in a sea of mist.

Every once in a while, they went through a tunnel, and their phones would lose signal. This meant the lecture Dr. Simone was listening to through the car's audio system would pause. The inside of the car would be eerily silent as they emerged on the other side into a new cloud of fog. Shelby felt absolutely certain that the hills were enchanted and daydreamed of the creatures she could meet there.

Waiting for her parents to finish their meeting at the university had been a little less enjoyable. In theory, everything was great. She'd packed several books to read, her sketchbook and some pencils if she felt like drawing, and a little snack. She knew it was going to be a few hours, and she was definitely aware of how long an hour could feel, so she debated bringing her tablet. She decided not to. *It would be too awkward to ask for the WiFi password, anyway,* she thought to herself.

Her parents had left her in the waiting room for the university's Anthropology Building. Apparently, the department admin had reserved a private work room for Shelby to hang out in while her parents were in their meeting, but there seemed to be a problem. The admin had gone directly to the facilities office to deal with it.

In the meantime, that meant Shelby was sitting very quietly in a very academic waiting room. Most of the waiting room was taken up by the admin's huge desk, which looked incredibly old. Shelby felt it looked appropriate in an anthropology building and wondered which professor had insisted on it being used.

The only seats were carved wooden cubes that looked really cool to Shelby but were uncomfortable to sit on. She struggled to find a position that didn't make her rear end hurt.

Thankfully, there was also a large stack of *National Geographic* magazines piled on top of what seemed to be a large tribal drum. Shelby could appreciate the decor. They had a wall of ceremonial masks in their dining room at home, each gifted to the Simones during their excavations.

Shelby found it hard to concentrate on her book. *This one didn't even have horses in it,* she thought with disgust. Still, her father had said that Treasure Island was one of his favorite books when he was her age, so she was determined to get through it.

After a few minutes of constantly trying to find a comfortable reading position on the wooden cube, a flustered older woman burst into the room. Her face was red; her gray hair was frizzy and untamed; and her outfit, which should have looked stunning on her, was rumpled. Shelby immediately liked her.

Miss Laurel, as she introduced herself, was the admin for the Anthropology Department, and she was so very sorry Shelby had had to entertain herself while she was gone. She showed Shelby into a private work room, which was basically a small room with a desk, a chair, and a glass wall with a door that closed.

"These are for students to use, but I made sure you could borrow one. Typically, we don't allow food and drink in here," she said, pointing at the sign. "But you don't look like the kind to make a big mess, are you?"

"No ma'am," Shelby replied. "I've just got water, grapes, and crackers with me. But I don't have to eat them here."

"Nonsense," Miss Laurel said. "If you're going to be stuck here for a few hours, you might as well have a good time. Please just don't make a mess."

Shelby swore she wouldn't, and Miss Laurel finished getting her settled in. "Also, all of the snacks in the breakroom are up for grabs. The breakroom is right next to the bathrooms, just down this hall in front of you. Super convenient. I figured you wouldn't want to ask for directions every time you needed anything. But, if you do, just holler."

With a grin, Shelby thanked Miss Laurel as she left, shutting the door behind her. The glass wall let in a lot of light, so Shelby didn't bother turning on the light in the room. Instead, she pulled out her book and tried again to concentrate on the adventures of Jim Hawkins.

Jim, Captain Smollett, and the crew of the *Hispaniola* were underway when Shelby decided it was time for a stretch break. She wandered to the break room, where she found a lemon sparkling water that looked interesting. Remembering that the snacks were *up for grabs*, she spirited them away to her meeting room, where she pulled out her sketch pad for something different.

Shelby didn't know exactly how much time passed, but she was busy sketching a school of mer-ponies surrounding what Shelby hoped was recognizable as a schooner. She'd seen pictures before and read Robert Louis Stevenson's description in *Treasure Island*, but she had to admit that she was basically guessing. Just as she was developing a frown of self-doubt about her artwork, Shelby's parents waved from the other side of the glass door.

"What are you doing here in the dark, Sport?" Shelby's dad swung the door open. "I can barely see you back there!"

"Cool hyperbole, Dad, but I'm right here." Shelby carefully closed her sketchbook so her drawing wouldn't smudge and stowed all of her supplies in her backpack.

Her dad chuckled. "Alright, alright. Weak effort. What can I say? I think I just used the phrase DNA evidence three hundred times in a row in that meeting. I'm losing my marbles." He made a silly face at Shelby, who giggled.

"How about we grab a nosh, and then meander to this tack emporium?" Shelby's dad asked.

"I could masticate some sustenance," Shelby replied. "But I'd rather navigate to the tack emporium without deviation."

Shelby's dad nodded approval, "Your vocabulary skills are simply..." he searched for just the right word and finished with, "cool".

"COOL?" Shelby yelped and immediately clapped her hands over her mouth. She'd forgotten where they were.

Shelby's mom rolled her eyes. "You two and your word games. Can't take you anywhere." As she fished her car keys out of her satchel, she continued, "And you absolutely can't go shopping on an empty stomach, Shelby. We're going to stop at an Ethiopian place Professor Lopez recommended. I can't believe they have Ethiopian in this..." She gestured around her at the seemingly suburban area.

"Three-horse town?" Shelby's dad suggested. "Bigger than a one-horse town, but not quite a full stagecoach team?"

"In the car, now," Shelby's mom insisted with a stern look on her face, but Shelby knew she was kidding. Plus, she was excited to have some Ethiopian food. It had been a long time since she had had anything more exotic than the pasta dishes at Pasquale's, which was Old Quarry Lake's only pizza place.

After eating a regrettable amount of delightfully spiced dishes and pancake-like injera, Shelby wanted to take a nap more than she wanted to shop. Still, a stop at HorsePro Tack Emporium would be the highlight of their day.

When they arrived, Shelby was almost nervous to go inside. Compared to Marian's tack shop in Old Quarry Lake, this place was humongous.

The Simones walked through the automatic doors into a sea of riding clothing, tack, and horse supplies. Horse blankets of all sizes draped an entire wall.

Shelby didn't realize she was staring until her father's voice surprised her. "Sport? Earth to Old Sport? Do you read us?"

"Yeah. Um... yes," Shelby realized she sounded dazed. "This is just a lot of..."

"Stinky horse stuff?" her father finished for her. "You bet. Of course, it's not exactly stinky yet. But the pervasive leather aroma is undeniable."

Shelby's mom rolled her eyes. "Shelby and I know what to do. We're old pros at this. Come on, Shelby, it looks like the ladies' riding tights are over here."

Mrs. Simone took her daughter by the hand and gently guided her through the maze of clothing racks and shoppers at the front of the store. Soon, they were standing in front of a rack of pants that Shelby recognized from Marian's shop.

Shelby had the disadvantage of being a still-growing kid of average height with a larger-than-average waist size. On her first trip to the tack shop in Old Quarry Lake, Shelby, and Marian had discovered that ladies' riding tights were great for Shelby's shape. Riding tights were similar to regular leggings, only they were specifically designed for saddle duty with carefully placed seams and grippy patches.

"Can I help you find something in particular?" The voice that came from behind Shelby startled her, and she jumped a little, knocking a pair of tights off their hanger. She fumbled with the tights for a moment, then turned around. Her face felt hot, and she knew she was blushing. "Hi. Sorry. I'm sorry. Yes?" Shelby stammered out.

Thankfully, her mom was right behind her. "Hi there," Dr. Simone said to the salesperson. "My daughter is starting horse camp this week, and we need a few pairs of breeches for her. She already has these tights, so I guess we're looking for a few more pairs."

The salesperson stared at Shelby in a way that made her feel like one of her parents' microscope slides.

"Are you new to riding? Is this your first time?" The question felt cold, and Shelby couldn't figure out how to answer it.

"Actually, she's been riding for a while," Shelby's mom replied. "School is delayed this year, so we've got an extra opportunity for horse camp. This will be her first horse camp, though, so we're looking for something that can deal with being washed and worn a lot. Do you have any recommendations?"

"Okay, so this is the ladies' section. That means it's for grown-ups. But our kids' sizes only run extra small through large in the store itself. You can order *extended sizes* on our website. They can ship them to the store so you can pick them up at no extra charge." The sales associate said the words in a hushed tone like they were a secret.

"Unfortunately, we don't live here in town, so we'd probably just have to pay shipping. Do you have any samples of those extended sizes in the store to try on? She's been wearing the medium in the MountUp tights. Do you have that brand?" Shelby could tell that her mother took offense to the salesperson's insult, but she didn't miss a beat.

"We really don't need *extended sizes* in the store. And we carry exclusively high-quality HorsePro brands," the salesperson said in that same whispery voice, gesturing around to the aisles of shoppers. Shelby suddenly became very aware that she was the only person in the store who could identify with *extended sizes*.

"Oh. How disappointing," Shelby's mother said in a flat, even voice. "Well, come on Shelby. Nothing to see here." With her hand on her daughter's shoulder, Shelby's mom guided her towards the entrance.

Somewhere in their journey, Shelby's dad reappeared, wearing a cowboy hat and carrying a whip. "Ta-da! Indiana Jones," He announced triumphantly.

"Stan put that back. They don't have anything here." Shelby's mom sounded angry, and Shelby's stomach started to flip-flop a little. Was she in trouble? She didn't think she had done anything wrong, but her mother had never dragged her out of a store before.

"For Halloween, though?" Shelby's dad sounded defeated, but also hung the hat and whip on the display he got them from and followed them to the parking lot.

Shelby's mom stormed to the car in silence. Shelby's dad followed, confused, while Shelby tried to remember what she had done wrong to make her mother so mad.

Finally, her mom turned around. "Shelby, I want you to know that I don't care what size or shape you are. You are a beautiful person no matter what. As long as you don't have the attitude of that vile person, I don't care." Shelby's mom looked like she was about to cry.

"What is going on?" Shelby's dad asked. "I turn into Indiana Jones for two minutes..."

Shelby's mom turned to face him. "They don't have *extended sizes*, Stan." She repeated *extended sizes* with the same understated sneer the salesperson had used. Shelby had to smile. That tone made it completely clear who her mom was *actually* angry at.

"Well, that's gross," said Stan Simone. The master wordsmith was at a loss for words. "But if we leave now, we'll have time for a movie before bedtime arrives. Or we can see what the History Channel has to offer?"

Without saying another word, the Simone family got in their car and drove away from HorsePro Tack Emporium.

Shelby's Diary

I don't understand why people need to be mean, Diary. I was so excited to go to my first big tack shop, and I barely got to see anything. The salesperson basically told Mom and me that I was too fat to ride. Okay, so I was bloated from eating too much injera. Okay, so I'm not a teeny-tiny little rider girl. I'm still a rider.

Luckily, Mom had it all under control. I didn't even have time to embarrass myself by blushing, crying, or doing something awkward because Mom marched me right out of there before I even realized she was being mean. Diary, this evil salesperson made me feel awful. The whole ride home I felt like I was bigger than the moon.

As Dad drove us home, Mom texted Bill for some ideas. He actually called us instead. He said it was too much to type on the stupid little keys. Thanks to the power of the phone connection thingy in the car, we could all hear him. I even jotted down a few ideas on my sketch pad. I should have brought a notebook, too, but in hindsight, I guess.

Anyway, Bill Radnor is the greatest person on Earth, Diary. He said he knew how terrible shopping for breeches could be. I forgot that he spent a few years riding jumpers when he was younger.

Bill also knows what it's like to be a rounder person than average. I tried talking to Katherine and Rose about my trip in our group chat, but they both love HorsePro. They don't need the "extended sizes." Diary, I wish you had heard this nasty person say extended sizes like it was some kind of disease.

But Bill gave me a few online stores to try out. He said he would talk to Marian, too, about whether she could get some pants for us short-round types shipped to the store so I could get them in time for camp. I really like the pants I got at her store, so that's a pretty good plan. Even if they aren't high-quality. I hope you can hear my eyes roll, Diary.

I hate the fact that everything has to be so difficult. I wish I was normal-sized. Whatever the normal size? Mom said she was chubby like me until she went to college, and then everything just evened out, as she says. I never really thought about it much until I started riding, but that's why I'm so glad I know Bill. He knows that round people can still belong on a horse.

Anyway, I need to get to bed, Diary. Tomorrow is my first day of horse camp... even though I won't have new breeches to wear. Good grief.

Chapter Six

First Day of Camp Blues

Shelby woke up the next morning with a feeling in her tummy that she was going to have a bad day. But she remembered one of Bill's favorite sayings when coaching Rose and Whisper over the big fences: "If you think 'OH NO!' then 'OH NO!' is exactly what's going to happen." What he meant was that if you make up your mind that bad things are going to happen, then they will.

So, Shelby tried to pretend those feelings weren't there. She ate some oatmeal, got dressed, and brushed her teeth just like she would any other day. Of course, on this particular day, she was up two hours earlier than normal and actively ignoring a terrible all-over nervous feeling, but she did not stray from her routine.

Shelby grabbed her snack bag, which had a couple of extra water bottles in it, as well as a hummus sandwich and raw veggies for lunch. Shelby was absolutely certain that wouldn't make her popular with the rest of the campers, but she was still looking forward to it.

Hopping in the car with Katherine and Drew, Shelby noticed right away that they were both far more silent than usual. Immediately, Shelby wondered if it was because of horse camp.

"I'm sorry," she blurted out.

Katherine looked startled. "Sorry about what? Sorry about the fact that my butt-face brother thinks he's entitled to the last Pop-Tart, thus depriving his favorite little sister of anything at all for breakfast. Sorry about the fact that he then was busy texting his robot girlfriend and didn't have time to stop at the gas station to buy her a Pop-Tart to make up for it. Your esteemed sister would have also accepted a dollar granola bar, but no," she said, drawing the word out dramatically, "We have to tell a robot she looks cute."

Drew snorted as he pulled the car out of the Simones' driveway. "Yeah, the Pop-Tart thing was a butt-face move, but it was a mistake. I thought there was another pack in there."

"And what about wasting my time with that fake girlfriend?" Katherine folded her arms across her chest.

"Ok, for the last time, I'm beta testing an AI application that allows teenagers to interact with other teens around the world in a safe, creeper-free zone." Drew's tone was sharp.

Shelby took a deep breath. Katherine and Drew rarely fought, but when they did, it was usually short and brutal. She drifted off into her own little world while the two of them snapped at each other. She imagined a horse running alongside the car as they drove towards the barn. Her imaginary horse jumped ditches, fences, shrubs, and driveways as they whizzed past them.

In fact, her imaginary horse had just cleared an impressive slatted fence when Shelby realized they were at the edge of the Old Quarry Lake Farms property. She also noticed that it was incredibly quiet in the car.

"I have an extra cereal bar that my mom packed as a snack," Shelby offered up helpfully. She hoped her timing was right. Sometimes when she wasn't paying close attention, she could say things at the wrong time and make everything awkward.

"Thank you, Shelby," Katherine said in a pointed tone. "I would love to enjoy your cereal bar. Eating first thing in the morning is very important to me." She unwrapped the bar and took a large bite. "I'm buying my lunch today, so I will happily let you have the granola bar from my lunch to repay you." She shoved the entire cereal bar in her mouth without breaking eye contact with Drew in the rearview mirror.

This wasn't the first time Shelby had been confused by how siblings behaved with each other, and she was certain it wouldn't be the last, either. Sometimes she thought she was missing out by not having a brother or sister, but moments like this reminded her of the benefits of being an only child.

As Shelby stepped out of the car, she couldn't help but notice that the yucky nervous feeling was still there. She didn't feel sick to her tummy or dizzy, but more like everything was wrong all at once. She wanted very much to go back to bed and pull the covers over her head. But it was the first day of horse camp, and she knew she should be excited.

Upon arriving at the barn, each of the different camp groups met in different places. The Green group met at the end of Aisle F, so Shelby and Katherine headed in that direction.

"I'm sorry my brother is a butt-face," Katherine grumped as they walked. "But seriously, thank you for the cereal bar. That was clutch. My tummy needs breakfast, or I get super hungry."

"No problem," Shelby said. "I don't actually like those, but they have the least amount of sugar, so my mom keeps buying them. I've got you covered." They both giggled.

The first thing each group did was introduce themselves to each other and share their favorite thing about the horse they rode in their lessons. Bill started, naming Lil' Sugar's kind attitude as his favorite thing about her. "But don't look at her wrong in the show pen, or she'll tell you all about it," he concluded. The students laughed.

As the students went around in a group, Shelby practiced what she was going to say. She hated being put on the spot, so she thought carefully about what she wanted to say about Coins.

But then the shorter blond boy standing next to Shelby piped up. "I'm Thomas," he said. "You can call me Tom, but most people call me Thomas. I just turned eight. I like Buddy because he has an incredible canter."

Shelby did a double-take. Eight years old? Buddy? Cantering? Shelby understood the words, but together they just didn't make sense. This kid could get Buddy to move? He was probably a good three inches shorter than Shelby.

Once again, Shelby was aware of too much attention being paid to her. She looked around and just as she feared, everyone was staring at her.

Bill was smiling, though, and the other members of the Green group were looking more bored than annoyed at the pause Shelby had created. Katherine flashed her a quick thumbs-up. *Oh good,* Shelby thought. *I can pretend it's stage fright instead of not paying attention.*

"I'm Coins, and I like Shelby," she announced quickly. Too quickly, she realized. She'd gotten that all wrong. Her face was growing hot as she blushed, and that nervous feeling got stronger. She felt kind of shaky, just like when she'd seen the camp placements.

Naturally, all of the kids were laughing at her mistake. Some of them were laughing a little harder than Shelby felt was appropriate, too.

"Nice to meet you, Coins," Thomas said with a cruel smile. "Which stall is yours?" Shelby looked at her feet in embarrassment.

Bill got everyone to hush after a minute and looked at Shelby warmly. "Now go ahead and run us through that again, Miss." He tipped his cowboy hat again.

Bill's the best, Shelby thought for what she figured was the ten millionth time. She took a deep breath, let it out slowly, and tried again. "Hi, I'm Shelby. I like riding Coins because he's so patient with me when I lose focus. Just like Bill."

Katherine, Bill, and the other student counselors laughed this time, but Shelby could tell her little joke went over the younger kids' heads.

The counselors introduced themselves next. Mark and Brianne were older teenagers who had ridden at Bill's barn for many years. Mark was obsessed with barrel racing, like Bill, and was searching for the perfect next-level horse. Bill was letting him practice with Lil' Sugar in the meantime. Brianne was just starting to teach her off-the-track Thoroughbred Mega about jumping. She had gotten him just a few months earlier at a racehorse dispersal sale and had high hopes for making him a show jumper. Both counselors agreed that their horse's attitude was their favorite thing about them.

Katherine introduced herself as a Junior Counselor. "But my favorite thing about my horse Whisper is her slow jog. You can laugh about Quarter Horses having slow trots, but that jog makes me super happy."

With introductions over, Bill explained that the groups rotated where they were in the barn to avoid running into each other. The Green group would start the day riding, then go to the view room for horse care lessons. After that, everyone would head to a bay of picnic tables set up outside the barn for lunch. There would be hands-on demonstrations after lunch then the Green group would get their second ride of the day.

Shelby barely heard his instructions. She was already thinking too hard about what had just happened. *First impressions are everything,* she thought, *and I've just made the worst one possible.*

After stashing her lunch and snack bag in the Aisle F tack room refrigerator along with the other students, she gathered up Coins' tack. She loved the buttery soft leather of the English saddle she rode in. Gathering up the reins and straps of the bridle, she headed back to the aisle, where Bill had placed Coins in the cross-ties for her.

Shelby's first step was to hoist the saddle, saddle pad, girth, and bridle onto one of the built-in saddle racks along the aisleway. All the racks closest to Coins were taken with other students' gear, so she had to settle for one that was a few stalls away from where the spotted horse was standing.

Except she didn't quite get that far. She raised the saddle to place it on top of the rack, only for the bridle she'd placed on top to slide down onto her face. Shelby jerked her head and felt the reins slide down her back. She took a step backward to find her balance and stepped on the reins. With a yelp, she dropped everything on the ground.

The pony standing next to her in the crossties didn't exactly spook at the racket she was making next to him, but he stepped sideways quickly. To make matters worse, he stepped directly on the foot of the kid who was grooming him, who also yelped and dropped everything. Behind them, another pony tossed his head in surprise and pranced nervously in the crossties.

As if she was in a horrible dream, Shelby watched as each of her fellow campers' horses reacted in some way to the situation. None of them did anything terribly naughty, but all the campers looked shaken.

Katherine hurried up to Shelby, grabbing her tack. "Oops!" Katherine said with a patient chuckle. "Looks like the horses weren't ready for that." She easily scooped up Shelby's tack and placed it correctly on the saddle rack. Shelby tried to stammer out a thank you, but her mouth felt frozen.

Katherine laughed it off, though. "Go groom that horse of yours," she said patiently. "We've all dropped our stuff at some point. Sometimes gravity gets us!" She winked and headed off to help the students.

Shelby's body kept refusing to cooperate, though. She dropped the curry comb under Coins several times, and then unthinkingly bent over to pick it up. This caused Mark to give a hasty impromptu lesson to the students about how it's very important to never purposefully put yourself under a horse, as Shelby just had. Shelby was mentally face-palming.

The more she tried, the worse it got. She dropped the girth twice. Without the girth to secure it, Coins shook the saddle off onto the ground. "You're mocking me," she said out loud to the horse. "Try to help me out here. We want people to think we're cool, Coins."

Coins just snorted.

Eventually, Shelby got into the riding arena. All the other kids were already mounted up and riding.

"Door," Shelby called, as she led Coins through the opening to the arena. Bill had taught them all that doing this was important so the horses in the arena wouldn't spook at a newcomer. Now that Shelby knew what a spook felt like, she didn't want it to happen to anyone else.

Unfortunately, she simply hadn't seen Thomas walking Buddy directly towards them. She jerked Coins to a stop just as Thomas stopped Buddy. Thomas said nothing but rolled his eyes at Shelby. Shelby's heart sank. *Just one big mistake after another,* she thought to herself.

The morning ride was the highlight of Shelby's day. Coins lived up to expectations and carried Shelby around safely. They did some trot off of the lunge line, and Shelby was able to post a few strides without feeling like she was going to fall off. When she was on a horse, Shelby didn't feel awkward or self-conscious. She felt like she was flying.

The rest of the day, however, just got worse and worse. Shelby definitely had a case of what her mom called *the drops*. It seemed like every time she tried to pick something up, it fell. She dropped her pencil at least six times during the lesson about hoof anatomy and care. Her lunch tumbled out of the bag when she removed it from the fridge, sending baby carrots rolling in every direction in the tack room. Bill told her not to worry about it. "If the barn cats don't find them, I'm sure the night critters will."

To make matters worse, Shelby and Katherine didn't get to hang out at lunch. Katherine was busy preparing for the after-lunch demonstration, which was about braiding a horse's mane and tail for the show ring.

All the kids in the Green group knew each other already. The rest of the Green group was gathered around Thomas, listening to him tell stories about all of his accomplishments on horseback. Normally, Shelby would be interested, but something about Thomas irritated her. *Why don't you go canter Buddy with the Junior group and let the rest of us try to figure out the posting trot?* she wondered to herself.

When the Simone family moved, Shelby learned right away that everyone in Old Quarry Lake knew everyone. She knew that she was the new girl, and that was a strange thing in this small town.

At least it's better than being the horse girl, Shelby said to herself. Back in the city, the other students at her school had nicknamed her after her obsession with horses. But here, especially at Bill's farm, being a horse girl was just fine.

Still, as Shelby ate her hummus sandwich and remaining veggies alone at the end of a picnic table, she couldn't help but be excited for the afternoon and another ride!

Except the afternoon didn't turn out exactly as Shelby planned. During the braiding demonstration, she had managed to get Petey the pony's mane completely tangled. She tripped over absolutely nothing and knocked over Katherine's carefully laid-out display of combs and teeny-tiny braiding bands. Shelby yelped at the sight of the little rubber bands scattering all over the arena, where they would be forever lost in the dust. Her yelp startled Petey, who stepped on Thomas's foot.

"Twice? Twice in one day?" Katherine's voice was sharp.

"First time standing up?" Thomas asked her, his eyes narrowed and glaring.

SHELBY'S HORSE-FILLED SUMMER:

"I'm... I'm sorry. Sorry!" Shelby's voice and hands were shaking. She couldn't believe how clumsy she was being. She'd even made Katherine yell at her! Shelby felt big tears welling up in her eyes. She definitely didn't want to draw any more attention to herself, so she excused herself to the restroom and ran quickly in the direction of the view room to hide for the rest of forever... or at least until she could get her emotions under control.

Shelby's Diary

Diary, there's a saying: If I didn't have bad luck, I'd have no luck at all.

They wrote that about me. I know they did.

I showed up at horse camp today and made sure everyone knew how awkward weird and dumb I am. I dropped everything. I spooked all the horses. I caused two kids to get stepped on, even though the second one was stupid Thomas. Stupid Thomas does everything right. He's probably never been stepped on before. He's busy cantering and jumping and stupid stuff like that, even though he's only 8.

Katherine was sooooooooooo mad, Diary. She kept having to clean up after me. She didn't speak to me the whole way home. I kept trying to apologize, but she said, "Don't sweat it. Tomorrow is another day," and left it at that. She and Drew were still fighting when he picked us up, so we rode all the way home in silence. It was so creepy, Diary. I just wanted to cry. She wasn't even in the group chat tonight. Rose asked how the first day went, but I didn't want to answer without Katherine, so I just said, "I'm still as awkward as ever!" Rose said LOL, but that's it. Nothing else.

Why am I so stupid, Diary? Why can't I just get myself under control and do all the things I know how to do? Instead, I have to drop things make loud noises, knock things over, and waste ALL of Katherine's braiding bands.

On the plus side, Mom stopped at the tack shop on her way home from picking up pizza, and Marian ordered some of the riding tights Bill recommended for me. She also picked up some braiding bands to give to Katherine, so I can replace the ones that are now living in the arena. She's taking that part out of my allowance.

I'm not sure horse camp was such a good idea, Diary. I'm not sure anything I do is a good idea. I don't even know what I can do to make any of this better. Maybe Katherine is right, and tomorrow is another day to try again.

Chapter Seven

Camp Days Continue

Much to Shelby's delight, the second day of camp was better than the first. Katherine was thrilled that Shelby had replaced her braiding bands and gave her a big hug.

"I'm sorry I was cranky with you yesterday," she said. "It took me forever to set up that braiding demonstration. Mark and Brianne were too busy flirting with each other to help, and then once I was done, they had the nerve to tell me I'd done it all wrong! I had to talk to Bill about it, and then I felt like a snitch... anyway, I think we both had a rough start to camp.

"I have something for you, too," Katherine said with a smile. She handed Shelby a packet of Pop-Tarts. "It's not the same as a granola bar, but I thank you all the same."

Shelby grinned. Her mom thought Pop-Tarts were gross, so they hardly ever had them at home. Shelby, on the other hand, liked them very much. "You have no idea how awesome this is. Thank you, Katherine!" And the girls hugged again. Drew simply rolled his eyes and drove on to the barn.

The rest of the day went well. Mark and Brianne made it a point to call on Shelby as much as possible. At first, Shelby was flattered. After all, she did know the answers. Then she realized that was why the counselors were calling on her. They didn't want to take the time for the rest of the group to make their guesses. Shelby felt a little guilty about it, but she didn't know what she could say anyway. Maybe she could bring it up with Katherine on the way home.

The biggest problem Shelby had all day was posting the trot on Coins. Coins had a nice, smooth trot, which made it comfortable to sit. By letting her hips sway with the rhythm of Coins' legs moving forward and back, she could trot Coins and feel comfortable just sitting there.

But many riders of all disciplines practiced the posting trot to encourage their horses to move forward through their shoulders as they trot. To post, Shelby needed to let the momentum of Coins' trot lift her slightly out of the saddle each time the front leg that was closest to the wall went forward.

Shelby was familiar with watching Coins' shoulder move forward, and she knew when to rise out of the saddle. Unfortunately, Coins didn't really give her much momentum to help her rise, so she found herself straining to get her bottom out of the saddle just in time to sit again. As a result, she would post mightily, then lose her balance and flop onto Coins' back. Coins would kindly slow down to a walk so she could gain her balance again, but then she would be flustered and have to ask for the trot again. She was getting frustrated, and she could tell Coins was getting frustrated with her.

Shelby's legs also weren't used to riding twice a day, every day, so by the time they got to the second ride of the second day, she couldn't even trot the patterns Bill had laid out for the students. Thankfully, Bill understood completely, and let her ride at a walk.

Thomas, of course, had never been sore from riding. As Shelby finished weaving Coins through some cones at a walk and joined the other students at the end of the arena, Thomas called to her out from Buddy's back. "We're going to call you Tick-Tock instead of New Girl because you like to take your time." The other students laughed like this was the cleverest thing they had ever heard.

"And we're going to call you Impatient." Bill was standing nearby and overheard the whole thing. Shelby blushed. "That was a great course, Shelby," Bill continued. "And it brings to mind the importance of schooling exercises at the walk. We're going to do the rest of the lesson in a nice, forward, steady walk. I want rhythm; I want balance, and I don't want to see your horse fussing."

Shelby looked over at Katherine, who was standing with the other counselors. Katherine was grinning and flashed her the thumbs-up sign. Shelby didn't feel very thumbs-up worthy, but she appreciated her friend's vote of confidence.

On the way home from horse camp that night, Katherine listened and sympathized as Shelby wailed about the posting trot.

"It's not just you," Katherine said soothingly. "Everyone struggles with it, and Coins isn't helping you. I could fall asleep to his nice steady jog."

Shelby rolled her eyes, "I bet Thomas was posting Buddy's trot within thirty seconds of meeting him."

"Thomas fell off Buddy the first time he rode him because he wasn't paying attention to where he was going and steered him straight into another student," Katherine replied, matter-of-factly.

Shelby was shocked. "What?" She had to make sure she had heard Katherine correctly.

"Thomas thinks he's important because his parents are rich, and he's done a lot of cool stuff for his age. But he's also eight years old, doesn't have his own horse, and failed the written test. Don't worry about him," Katherine said confidently. "If you want, I can hang out at the end of the arena tomorrow and try to give you some pointers as you go by."

"I don't think there's anything that can save me," Shelby moaned. "I think I'm just doomed to bobble around on the back of a horse like a rubber ducky for all of eternity."

The image made both of them laugh. The rotten first day of camp had been put behind them after all.

Shelby's Diary

Dear Diary,

I can't post the trot, and Thomas is a rude little boy.

That's all.

Love,
Shelby

Just kidding, Diary. I can't let you off that easy. I have problems, but they're the same problems I've had all week. I just can't seem to get the hang of posting the trot. Bill has tried to help. Katherine is going to try to help me. I am just helpless. Cannot be helped.

How can someone try so hard to do something right, and it just not happen? It's just not fair.

On the other hand, maybe I'm not meant to post the trot. Posting isn't required for a lot of equestrian sports. I can't think of any right now, but I'm sure there are ways to get around it.

I would also like to talk about Thomas, Diary. Wow. What a brat. I got the scoop on him on the way home from camp. Apparently, his parents own the only insurance agency in town, so they're mega-rich and everyone loves them. But pretty much everyone thinks Thomas is a little jerk—that's according to Drew.

He's not a bad rider, really. He and Buddy seem to enjoy each other. Thomas is just really impatient and likes to yell at me. It's not even his job to yell at me. Drew came in with the truth bomb on that one, too. When Katherine and I were talking in the car, he said, "You pay Bill to tell you about your riding, not that little jerk, Thomas." That's how it came up.

I know he's not the absolute best rider ever, and I should ignore him. My parents say that sometimes it's easy for kids to make fun of me because I wear my heart on my sleeve and follow my dreams. I'm not entirely sure what that means, but I think it means that Thomas is only making fun of me because it isn't hard to find something to make fun of. I'm a fat kid with big hair who can't post the trot.

But then again, at least I'm not a little jerk. Maybe I should talk to Bill about it. I know he can hear most of the stuff Thomas says, and he's really good at having my back. Which I love. But I don't understand why someone would want to be angry and mean when all they have to do is pay attention to their own horse.

None of the other kids in our group have said much to me at all, beyond camp stuff. They worship the ground Thomas walks on, though. I don't want to be as popular as Thomas. I just want him to be quiet and ride Buddy and ignore me.

I can't believe camp is almost halfway over. I've actually learned so much—a little bit about horse care and body parts, but mostly about what it means to be a good horse person. I can't wait to see what the rest of the week brings... even if it means dealing with Thomas and flopping around at the trot.

Chapter Eight

Sit Up, Relax, and Ride

On the third day of horse camp, Shelby pulled on her brand-new riding pants and attempted to face the day with a little more confidence. *Today you will post the trot. It's no big deal. You will trot. You will post. You, Shelby Simone, will figure it out,* she said to herself.

And yet Shelby still struggled with the posting trot. "Try getting Coins to move a little faster," Katherine encouraged her from the ground. "I know that doesn't make sense, but when he's moving more forward, his trot gets bigger, which will help you get out of the saddle."

So, Shelby tried to get Coins to move faster but only succeeded in making herself feel more tired. No matter how she kicked, the big spotted horse simply wouldn't trot faster than his nice, comfortable jog.

"Nice going, Tick-Tock," Thomas chortled as he sailed by on Buddy. "But it helps if you get your butt out of the saddle. All of it!"

Shelby choked back tears and walked Coins for the rest of the lesson.

After camp on the third day, Bill asked Shelby to stay a little bit, promising Katherine and Drew that he *wouldn't hold y'all up much*. Shelby loved the way Bill worded things. No one said *y'all* in the city.

In the view room, Bill asked Shelby calmly, "So what do you think is going on with this posting thing?"

Shelby blushed – a familiar sight to Bill by now. "You don't have to feel any particular way about it, Shelby, but I wondered what was going on in your head. I can see things from the ground, but I can't tell how you feel about things unless you tell me."

Before she knew it, Shelby heard herself telling Bill everything. How she couldn't get her bottom out of the saddle, how she lost the rhythm because she couldn't lift herself. She even told him about how Thomas being so much better than her made her feel sad about her own experience and what he had said about her riding.

Bill listened carefully, and once Shelby had told him everything, he nodded. "Yep. I don't know why Thomas is trying so hard to make sure you have a bad time, Shelby, but I want you to listen to me. He doesn't have control over what you think about yourself. He's a decent rider now, but trust me when I say he hasn't always been. We all start somewhere. I think I've told you that before."

"We're gonna try something tomorrow," Bill said. "I don't think you're going to like it, but you need to trust me." And with that, he let Shelby in on the plan. Shelby left the barn with a great big grin on her face.

"What was that all about?" Katherine asked as Shelby got in Drew's car.

"Posting trot stuff," Shelby said mysteriously. "Surprise tomorrow!" And she left it at that.

Shelby was nervous when she woke up on the fourth day of horse camp. This was a different type of nervous, though. It wasn't that weird dread she had experienced on the first day of camp. This was more like excitement.

The day went along normally. During the first ride of the day, Bill put Coins on the lunge line. He asked Coins to trot a little faster than Shelby necessarily enjoyed. But, as Katherine had promised, this faster trot helped her get her posting rhythm down. She found herself relaxing into the forward beat.

The day's lessons were about horse illnesses, including colic. Even if Shelby hadn't known about colic from her horse care books, she'd read about it in novels from *Black Beauty* on up. Colic was one of the most serious conditions a horse can get. Horses have very long intestines, and they can't vomit. So, when they get a stomachache due to something they ate, those intestines can get twisted, tangled, or even erupt. Most of the time, though, a colicking horse feels uncomfortable until they finish digesting whatever is blocking their system. Sometimes a vet can flush it out with fluids. But other times, horses need surgery to help them.

The idea of colic terrified Shelby. She couldn't imagine how horrible it would be to have a horse colicking. She felt scared and anxious about watching a horse suffer and not being able to make him feel better. She carefully put the thought out of her mind, though. She wouldn't have to worry about her own horse for a long time. There was no way she was ready for that responsibility!

Plus, there were more important things to worry about right now. Shelby was looking forward to the afternoon riding session when she and Bill would reveal their surprise. At the same time, thinking about what she was about to do woke up those butterflies in her tummy.

Don't worry about all that, she thought to herself. *Remember what Bill said about what other people say.*

Still, as they tacked up their horses for the afternoon riding lesson, Shelby felt a little clammy and nervous. *What if this turned out all wrong?* she thought. *Like that first day. I don't think I could live through that again!*

She finished putting Coins' bridle on, noting with satisfaction that Mark had to put Buddy's bridle on for Thomas. They led their horses to the arena, where Shelby made a point of standing next to Thomas and Buddy.

Bill entered the ring. "We're going to do something different today," he announced. "I want you to look at the person next to you. And then I want you to switch horses."

There was a shocked murmur among the riders. Everyone except Mark and Brianne seemed surprised.

Thomas looked at Shelby with a grimace. "Are you sure that's a good idea, Bill? My dad says liability insurance only covers so much stupidity."

Bill sauntered over to where they were standing. "That's saying a lot, Thomas. So, are you trying to tell me I'm stupid, or are you insulting Shelby here?"

It was Thomas's turn to blush, and Shelby hoped the look on his face would live in her memory forever. "Never mind," he stammered and shoved Buddy's reins into Bill's hands. He stormed over to Coins and took the reins from Shelby without saying a word.

"Alright, Shelby," Bill said. "Let me help you get on up, and I want you to remember everything we talked about. Everything."

Shelby had forgotten how massively big Buddy was. Still, as Bill helped her adjust her stirrups, she made herself relax, taking deep breaths and rolling her shoulders like he had shown her.

"Buddy, we're gonna make this work," she said confidently to the horse. Buddy flicked an ear but showed no sign of being bothered by the change in plans.

Bill approached Buddy's left shoulder to give Shelby a pep talk. "Just get him on the rail, and I want you to remember what I said about your hips. Just let him move them. It's going to feel scary, but I want you to trust him, me, and especially yourself on this. Just move!" He punctuated this last statement with a hard pat on Buddy's shoulder.

Shelby grinned. Now that she was up on Buddy's back, so far away from the ground, her stomach was feeling flip-floppy again. Then she looked over at Thomas, who was complaining about the saddle, the stirrup length, and the way Coins naturally stood. Her grin got a little wider. Shelby took a deep breath, gave her shoulders a little shake to loosen them up, and signaled Buddy to walk on. He walked on.

The rest of the ride was like the best dream ever. *Only this is real!* Shelby had to remind herself several times.

Shelby also had to remind herself to let her hips stay loose and not clench her hands on the reins. "Buddy isn't going to go any faster than he needs to. If you give him any reason to think you don't want to go forward, he's going to take you up on it. So, keep your seat relaxed, your hips relaxed, your arms relaxed, and most of all, keep your brain relaxed," Bill told her.

Shelby tried to breathe rhythmically with Buddy's walk, remembering the way Bill had taught her. *Four hoofbeats to a stride, one breath to a stride. Breathe IN, step, step, step. OUT, step, step, step.* She chanted along silently with the walk and her breath. *Brain... relax. Arms... relax. Butt... relax.* The last one made her smile to herself.

More importantly, it worked. As Shelby relaxed, Buddy relaxed with a snort, lowering his mighty neck and relaxing through his shoulders. Shelby found that his walk was really very comfortable... when she wasn't trying to fight the forward motion!

But then came the dreaded "t" word. As Bill asked the group to trot, Shelby felt her elbows clamp to her sides, and her seat clenched. Buddy immediately picked his neck up and shortened his stride.

In, step, step, step. Out, step, step, step. Brain... relax. Arms... relax. Butt... relax, Shelby reminded herself. And then she gently asked Buddy for a trot on the next exhale. Buddy trotted off. *In, step, step, step. Out, step, step, step. Brain... relax. Arms... relax. Butt... relax.* Shelby let Buddy move her hips from side to side and found it hard to sit. So, she started posting. She let her weight sink into her heels. *In, step, step, step. Out, step, step, step. Brain... relax. Arms... relax. Butt... relax.* She felt like she was flying way too fast, but she was doing it. She was posting Buddy's trot, all by herself!

"Let's bring it back to a walk." Shelby heard Bill announce to the group. She didn't know how long they had been trotting. Had it been thirty seconds or thirty minutes? Shelby had lost track of time again, but she couldn't stop grinning.

"Alright. And bring it on into the center. Thomas, I'm going to give you a chance to trot Coins without everyone in your way. Looks like he's not wanting to stay on the wall for you."

Shelby pulled on Buddy's reins so quickly that the big horse shook his head.

"Sorry, Buddy. That was really rude of me. But I've got to see this." Shelby encouraged Buddy into the center of the arena, halted him, and let him relax on a loose rein.

Thomas was struggling to keep Coins steering in a loop around the entire arena. Coins had what Bill and Shelby called "Wander-itis", meaning that unless his rider was providing clear steering instructions, he'd amble along at his own will. Shelby sympathized with Thomas's difficulty.

A little bit.

Finally, Thomas got Coins back along the inside wall of the arena. Looking angry under his helmet, Thomas gave Coins a big wallop of a kick. Coins snorted and started cantering. Shelby hadn't cantered Coins yet, but what she saw looked smooth and comfortable. Thomas wasn't having any trouble sitting it, but it was clear he was frustrated. He yanked back on the reins, shouting, "Trot!" Coins came to a rapid halt. Thomas stared at the group in frustration and wailed, "This thing is terrible!" He gave Coins a big kick, and Coins started trotting from a complete halt. Again, Thomas brought him to a halt so fast that Coins' back legs kicked up little clouds of dust.

Shelby felt a knot in her stomach. Thomas was being absolutely horrible, and she was embarrassed just to be here. Bill was able to calmly reply, though. "Well, he's actually giving you exactly what you're asking for. This is a pretty impressive horsemanship pattern you're showing us, Thomas, but all we really need is a trot."

Thomas was finally willing to listen, so Bill gently coached him through it. "Let go of his face," Bill started, referring to the tight grip Thomas had on the reins... which led directly to the bit in Coins' mouth. "Loosen up those arms. Give him a little bump to get him walking." Thomas didn't look like he was happy about it, but he did what Bill asked. "Great. Now when you're ready, just a little bump to go to trot."

The transition from walk to trot was decent, but Thomas started scowling again. "Is this a trot? Is this some kind of weird gait?" he asked.

"That's your trot!" said Bill, and with that, he instructed the rest of the group to join Thomas in trotting on the rail.

Thomas seemed to get the hang of the differences between Buddy and Coins after a bit, and Shelby learned to relax and enjoy Buddy's trot. She decided it wasn't that fast, after all. It was just super bouncy. *But,* she thought, *it's that extra bounce that makes posting that much easier.*

At the end of the session, Bill asked each of the riders what they learned by riding another horse. Most of the kids said they were surprised by how smooth, bouncy, hard to steer, or fast their new horse had felt. Thomas said, "I learned I don't like stock horses."

Katherine, who was standing behind him, rolled her eyes at Shelby. Appaloosas like Coins were considered stock horses, but so was Katherine's horse Comet. For that matter, so was Bill's quarter horse mare, Lil' Sugar.

When it was Shelby's turn, she said, "I learned that horses may be different and move differently, but they all want to be ridden quietly and confidently. So, you just need to figure out what's going on, sit up, relax, and ride!"

Bill got very quiet and stared at the ground for a minute. He looked up, "I like the way you said that, Shelby. That's what I'm trying to teach every rider who comes through this program. I want you all to understand horses– not just how to get them to trot or the difference between a lope and a canter. I want you to understand that horses are looking for communication, not just direction. We can tell them what we want, but they can always say no. And when you're arguing with something this size, there's a good chance you may not win that fight." Bill pointed at Buddy with his giant upright neck and wide body.

"A horse is a living, breathing critter. We can train them the best we can, but they're still real animals. They need our help taking care of them, and *we* need to listen to what *they* tell us they need. Whether that's in their stall, or when they're sick or lame, or when we're working with them. You're a team.

"Furthermore, that goes for every horse you work with. Buddy is no better than Coins, and Coins is no better than Lil' Sugar. Maybe better than Petey the pony, but Petey's got a nasty wicked little attitude." The campers laughed. Petey's mischievous shenanigans were popular tales around the barn.

"So, when you work with any horse—and I mean any horse—you've got to treat them with the same decency you do your favorite horse. You can't just get out there and cowboy around like you're in charge. You've got to figure them out. Sometimes it's easy. Sometimes you've got to take an extra lap or two to get everything organized," he said, gesturing to Thomas.

"The horse you are sitting on is the horse you're riding tomorrow. Can't wait to see you. Now go get untacked. We're going to learn about the role the horse's neck plays in its movement. Sounds boring, but we're going to watch a lot of action videos and have a snack, so bear with me," Bill finished and clapped his hands, signaling the end of the riding session.

Shelby dismounted slowly and carefully and gave Buddy a great big hug. "We've got this, Buddy," she said. And she meant it.

Shelby's Diary

Today was the best day ever, Diary.

First things first: I posted the trot!!!!!!!!!!!!!!

EVEN BETTER!!! It was on Buddy! Yes, that Buddy! From my placement testing! I know I shouldn't throw exclamation points around like glitter, but I'm just so excited Diary!!!!!

First of all, I didn't actually have a problem posting the trot. I really did get it. I thought I was just telling myself I understood it, but I really did. I just can't get out of the saddle on Coins the way I can with Buddy. And just like Katherine and Bill told me, it's a universal problem with Coins and his comfy trot. Even good old Thomas had a hard time posting the trot on Coins.

In fact, Diary. Thomas had a hard time doing EVERYTHING on Coins. He had a hard time steering. He couldn't figure out how to ask him to trot. Bill had to pull us all in the middle so Thomas could get it all figured out. And he did, so good for him. I think Coins was silently judging him, though.

I know that feeling good about this is petty, Diary, but here's the thing: Thomas has made me feel SO BAD. It's not that I'm exactly glad that he still struggles with some stuff. Like Bill says, everyone has their own way of learning. But I am glad to know that Thomas is still human and not some mega-super rider. He's an eight-year-old kid who rides just fine. His mouth is big, though, and he likes to use it.

I don't know a lot about bullies, Diary. We didn't really have them at Metro School for Girls. We had bratty girls, and girls who thought everyone was their personal butler or whatever, but no one was actually purposefully mean. Katherine said she would've wanted to slap Thomas every time he opened his mouth to say something. Rose—who finally stopped out during camp to say hi today, too!---said she'd happily shove him in the manure pile just for walking past her. I don't actually want her to do that, but I don't think I would stop her, either. Does that make me a terrible person, Diary?

Tomorrow is the last day of horse camp, which means it's the last time I have to deal with Thomas. That's pretty cool.

On the other hand, that means I'm going to have to find a new way to entertain myself. It's official: Old Quarry Lake School can't open for at least three more weeks due to all the stuff at the archaeological site. Apparently, some folks think it's my parent's fault, but they're just trying to protect the site and get the school open in a way that's safe for kids to be around. The last thing they want is a kindergartner wandering into a big open pit!

While we're on extra break, Rose and her family are going to go to their lake house. Sheriff Jensen came home early from work to get the car loaded and scoot out so they could watch the sunrise over the lake tomorrow morning. It's like a four-hour drive north, but she says it's super gorgeous up there. She asked us to keep an eye on Whisper while she's gone. Bill will take care of him, of course, but Katherine and I will make sure Whispie gets all the treats and scratchy scratches he needs.

Katherine and I are planning on hanging out at the barn as much as possible, but I think she's over me. We've had a really action-packed kind of week, Diary, so I don't blame her for wanting some Shelby-free time. I would love to hang out at the barn. Maybe I can figure out a way to go to the barn with her and not be annoying and drop everything! ARRRRGGGHH!

Chapter Nine

The Right Place at the Right Time!

Shelby could hardly believe it was the last day of horse camp. *Five days was hardly any time at all,* she thought as she walked into the barn.

The morning had started great. Shelby was still feeling pretty happy about everything that had happened the day before. Plus, her mom had changed her schedule at the dig site so she could take Shelby out for breakfast and drop her off at the barn for the last day. Shelby still had to wake up a little earlier than usual, but she was willing to do that if it meant yummy pancakes from the diner on the Old Quarry Lake square.

As Shelby dunked bites of her pancake in syrup, turning them carefully to get just the right amount of syrup into the pancake, she and her mom discussed all the things she had learned throughout the week. "It's been a good week," Shelby said in conclusion, "But I still feel like I'm just getting started. I'm in no way ready to own a horse," she finished.

"Well, that's great, sweetie, because your father and I are also in no way ready for you to own a horse," Dr. Simone's words sounded harsh, but she gave her daughter a warm smile over her coffee cup.

"I know," Shelby said with a mock moan. "Horses are stinky, scary death machines!"

"OK," said Shelby's mother. "I don't know if I'd go that far, but they're definitely not my favorite species. I know you love them, though, and I'm very proud of what you've learned and how much you're getting into this passion of yours. Now, if you're done with your breakfast, I can take you out to the barn. I know it's a little early, but I'm sure you can find something to entertain yourself with those stinky, scary... what was it you called them?"

Shelby grinned. "Adorable, fluffy, magical creatures who deserve all my love!"

A few moments later, Shelby was walking down the barn aisleway. There were still 30 minutes before camp officially started, so she was wandering around, looking for Bill. Maybe he would have some little chores she could help with before the other kids arrived.

Starting with Aisle A, she wandered through the barn. Occasionally, she stopped and patted one of the velvety horse noses that poked out over the stall doors to say hello. Each of the horses had a full water bucket and was happily munching on hay, so she assumed Bill had fed recently.

Soon she was in Aisle E, where Comet and Whisper's stalls were located. Comet came to her door the minute she heard Shelby's footsteps. She nickered warmly, checking to see if Shelby happened to have any treats for her.

"Sorry, girl," Shelby said, stroking the horse's soft nose. "No treats for you. Only love." Comet snuffled her a few times, then decided to turn her attention to her hay.

Shelby laughed. "I don't blame you. I prefer snacks to company sometimes, too!"

She turned to Whisper's stall. *Wait,* Shelby thought. *Where's Whisper?* She didn't see the big gray horse standing in his stall. She took a few steps closer. Maybe he was hiding in the back corner of his stall?

Then she saw him. Whisper was lying down on the floor of the stall. Shelby felt a lump rise in her throat. She knew that horses liked to lie down to sleep and rest, but this didn't look normal.

Whisper was covered in sweat and shavings from the floor of his stall. He was awake, but his eyes were wide. As Shelby watched, he rolled up onto his tummy with his legs tucked beside him and started nipping at his ribcage with his big teeth.

"Whisper, are you ok?" Shelby found herself speaking in a barely audible voice. Her throat felt very dry. She was very, very scared. "How you doing there, Whispie?"

The horse didn't acknowledge her. Instead, he stood up with a pained-sounding grunt. He paced this way and that way, then flung himself on the ground with another big grunt. He nipped at his belly a few more times, then lay flat with a loud sigh.

Oh no, Shelby thought to herself. *This is colic. This is not good! Where's Bill?*

Shelby quickly dashed through the aisles again to see if she'd missed him. She knew you should never run in a barn, but all of the horses were in their stalls. Besides, this was an actual emergency.

But Bill wasn't there. *Maybe he was up at the house,* Shelby thought hopefully. Looking out the tack room window, she didn't see his car in the driveway. Her heart sank. She felt very cold and very frightened.

Bill had shown each student where the emergency contact information was located. In the view room was a notebook that included phone numbers for the vet, the farrier, each of the trainers, the owners of the horses who boarded there, and of course, Bill himself.

Shelby picked up the phone in the view room and dialed Bill's cell phone number. He answered immediately.

"Uh, hello?" Bill's voice sounded suspicious. *He probably didn't expect a call from an empty barn,* Shelby thought.

"Hi, Bill, it's Shelby. Whisper is colicking what do I do?" The words came out in a rush.

"Shelby? Is that you? Who's colicking?" Bill's tone changed immediately.

"Whisper. He's lying on the floor of his stall, sweating, and thrashing around!" Shelby felt a cold sweat forming on her face and hands.

"Is he biting at his belly?"

She nodded, then remembered that Bill couldn't see her. "Yes!"

"Ok, Shelby, I'll be there in just a minute. I just ran up to the feed mill to get some stuff ordered. I'm on my way right now. Can you please call Dr. Iver from the contact info? You'll want to hit the option for emergency cases. Then I want you to go to Whisper's stall and watch him. Wait for me to show up, ok? I'll be right there."

Shelby hung up the phone and did as she was told. Dr. Iver was a very kind older man who didn't seem to mind getting phone calls at seven in the morning. He asked Shelby to tell him which horse was having trouble and to go monitor the horse and wait. "Don't let him get into any food right now. Remove any hay or grain if you can, but don't get hurt!"

Feeling as if she was in a nightmare, Shelby dashed back to Whisper's stall. The thoroughbred gelding was sitting somewhat upright again and stood when he heard Shelby approaching.

"Hey Whispie," she said softly. "I'm going to need to take some of your things while you're up." She pulled his feed dish out of his stall, noticing that it was still mostly full. "Oh, poor guy. You didn't even get to finish your breakfast."

Whisper stood in the corner of the stall, his head drooping towards the ground. He pawed his front feet in turns and occasionally nipped at his stomach.

Suddenly, Shelby remembered something from class. "If your horse is showing colic signs, one thing you can do to help them is walk them. This might get the horse's intestine moving again. Plus, it gives you something to focus on while you wait for the vet," Brianne had said. Brianne's horse had colicked right after she got him, and she explained that walking him in circles in the arena had kept both of them from panicking. "It's important that you keep them walking once you start, though, or they may try to lie down and roll. Lying down isn't bad, but thrashing and rolling is, so keep them moving."

Shelby grabbed Whisper's halter and lead rope from the front of the stall. She wasn't sure she should be doing this, but at the same time, not doing it seemed like an even worse idea. She slipped the thoroughbred's halter on and snapped the lead rope to the chin buckle.

"Let's go for a walk, Whispie," she said encouragingly. She pulled on the lead rope. Whisper groaned, and his knees buckled. For a minute, Shelby thought he was going to fall on her. With a lurch, they were out of the stall. Shelby reorganized the long lead rope and resumed her place at Whisper's head. "Alright. Walk time." She led Whisper down the aisle and around the corner to the arena.

Whisper tried to lie down every time Shelby paused walking, so she marched right along. As they walked, Shelby talked non-stop to the horse. "It's too bad your person is on vacation. She's at the lake," Shelby explained. "Sheriff Jensen was so happy to get another vacation. Humans work a lot more than horses do." She realized none of this made sense to Whisper, but she also knew that talking was keeping them both from becoming even more frightened.

So, she kept talking. She told Whisper about her challenges with the posting trot. She told Whisper about Thomas and how he made her feel. Shelby confided in Whisper like he was a sixteen-hand equine therapist.

After what felt like hours and miles of walking around and around in the arena, Bill came rushing in. "Alright. Dr. Iver is right behind me, getting his equipment out of the truck. How long have you been walking?"

Shelby blushed. She hadn't looked at the clock. But then she remembered. "Since I hung up with Dr. Iver. He said to take Whisper's food away from him, so I went right after our call."

"And you just decided to take Whisper for a walk?" Bill asked.

"Well, that was one of the things from the colic lesson," Shelby explained. She stepped backward uneasily. She had a sense that she was in trouble.

"You know this horse's reputation, Shelby," Bill said with a warning tone in his voice. "That probably wasn't the best idea, but it looks like it did a world of good for Whisper."

Shelby looked at the big gray horse. He was known for being naughty, sure, but not dangerous. And even more importantly, his breathing had slowed to a more normal rate. He wasn't sweating, either. Shelby thought he might even look a little perkier, too.

Bill collected the lead rope from Shelby and took Whisper back to his stall, where Dr. Iver was ready to examine him.

Dr. Iver took Whisper's pulse and temperature. He listened to Whisper's heart with his stethoscope, then listened to different spots on both sides of Whisper's belly.

After what seemed like forever, he glanced over at Bill and Shelby. "No doubt colic, but I think we've caught it just in time. I'm going to give Whisper a shot that will help him relax and help his intestines keep moving. Then I'll give him some fluids, and we'll see how he responds."

Bill nodded. "Shelby? Would you be so kind as to head back up to the front? I reckon the counselors are getting here about now. Could you tell them what's going on, and tell them to go ahead and get everyone started with the lesson part of this morning? I'm going to stay here with Dr. Iver and help with Whisper."

"Sure thing," she said breathlessly. She hadn't realized that she'd practically been holding her breath while Dr. Iver delivered his news. She gave Whisper a pat on the nose. "Whispie, I need you to be ok, understand? Rose is counting on you."

Bill chimed in. "Yeah, big guy. You're not supposed to do this when your family is out of town. Don't worry, Shelby. I'll call the Jensens next to let them know what's going on. Whisper's in good hands."

Shelby took off to the aisle to share Bill's message with the counselors. Her announcement was met with several cries of "Oh no!" or "Poor Whisper!" Each counselor vowed to stop by to check on Whisper throughout the day and then began to prepare for the first lesson of the day.

While the counselors were setting up, Katherine dashed over to Shelby. "Poor Whispie!" She looked like she was about to cry. "What happened?"

Shelby filled her in on how she had gotten to the barn early and everything that had happened since. It felt like it had been so long ago, but it hadn't even been an hour yet.

"And I think Bill's mad at me for walking Whisper on my own," Shelby concluded her tale.

Katherine scrunched up her face. "I mean, Whisper can be a little difficult to ride, but he's usually pretty sane when Rose works with him from the ground. I can see why he'd be worried about you just wandering around taking horses for walks. But you're right—that was exactly what we talked about during the colic session yesterday. And if I know Rose, she'll be more glad that you did walk him. After all, she did ask us to keep an eye on him!"

News spread quickly among the campers and counselors about Whisper's condition. Bill had to block off the aisle to prevent well-meaning students from crowding around the gray horse's stall. "We need to let him rest and get better,"

Bill explained. "I know you all want to cheer him on, but right now, he needs to chill out and relax. Let's just keep doing camp stuff and know that I'm keeping an eye on him. Dr. Iver can be out here lickety-split if anything happens."

Shelby couldn't help grinning at *lickety-split*. Bill had a certain vernacular, as her dad would say.

"And girls?" Bill directed this at Shelby and Katherine. "I figured you'd want to know that Rose and her dad are on their way back. The next 24 hours might be a little scary, so we're going to need to keep a close eye on Whisper all night."

"I'll help." Shelby raised her hand in the air like she was at school.

Katherine chimed in, "Me too. We can both stay tonight and take turns."

Bill smiled. "I'm sure glad Rose and Whisper have good friends like you two. But don't worry. I'm going to be doing most of the watching, along with Dr. Iver. You'll have your turn staying up all night when it's your horse that needs to be watched."

"Now, ladies. I suggest you get back to camp. Today is the Last Day Party, after all!"

Shelby's Diary

Wow, Diary. That was not the last day of camp I expected to have.

Yes, I got to ride Buddy again. Yes, it was a great ride again. Even better, Thomas refused to even try to post Coins' trot. Mark and Brianne weren't amused, either.

But the big story of the day, Diary, is that Whisper colicked! It was so scary. I was all alone in the barn when it happened, too. I don't actually remember doing it, but I called Bill and the vet. By myself. I was so scared for Whisper that I think I would have done anything!

Rose called me from her dad's cell phone at the barn. She called Katherine, too. Whisper is standing up, but he's not interested in food, and he hasn't, um, pooed yet. This could be a sign that he's still colicking, or that something bad happened in his guts when he was colicking. Or, as Dr. Iver said, it could just be everything working itself out naturally.

I wish horses could tell us what's wrong with them, so we wouldn't have to guess. However this morning, Whisper made it super clear that he didn't feel good. I kept thinking about what he looked like lying on the ground in his stall. It was horrible!

I feel like I won't sleep a wink tonight. I guess at least I can sleep in tomorrow, though. It's Saturday, and we don't have horse camp.

I really wanted to write about horse camp tonight, but I'm just super distracted by what happened with Whisper. I keep thinking about what might have happened if I hadn't wandered back there. No one really goes back to that aisle until the afternoon, unless it's on the way to one of the other parts of the barn. Would anyone have noticed that Whisper wasn't ok?

I can tell Katherine is taking it hard, too. On the way home from camp, she kept talking about "What if Comet colicked?" I get it. I was worried about my horse colicking, and I don't even have one!

I'm so scared for Rose, too. Whisper is her best friend. She would be totally lost without her horse!

I just hope Whisper is ok, Diary.

Chapter Ten

Whisper the Magic Pony

Shelby was sitting on Buddy's back. His giant, upright neck was in front of her. She was patting his weird, yellow-colored mane. Suddenly, she realized she didn't have the reins. Shelby looked around. There they were. The entire bridle had fallen off of Buddy's face, and it was lying in a heap around his feet. Shelby looked every which way. There was no one else in the arena.

This isn't safe, Shelby thought. She started to dismount, but as she started to slide down Buddy's left side, she realized that the arena floor was slithering with snakes! They covered Buddy's hooves and slid around on the bridle, which kept getting further and further away. Shelby yelped and scooted back up into the saddle. *What am I going to do?* She thought in a panic.

Then she noticed the snakes were making a weird noise. *Brrrrrrrrrrring!* said the snakes. They were all saying it at once. *Brrrrrrrrrrrrring!*

Shelby sat up with a jolt. She looked around for snakes, but there were none. She was safe and sound in her bed. *It was just a dream,* she thought with relief.

Then she jumped again. *Brrrrrrrrrrrrring!* The noise hadn't stopped. Now that she was awake, Shelby recognized that the house phone was ringing. They hardly ever got calls on that phone.

"Hello?" She heard her father answer the phone in the basement den. "Oh, hey there, Rose. Let me see if Shelby's up."

Shelby glanced at the clock on her bedstand. Did it really say 6:30? So much for sleeping in.

Then the events of the day before hit her and she gasped, "*Whisper!*" She flew down the stairs barefoot and whisked the phone out of her father's hand.

"Whoa there, Sport!" Shelby's dad exclaimed, but Shelby didn't hear him.

"Rose! I'm here!" she practically shouted into the phone.

Rose's voice came back equally loud through the phone, "He's fine, Shelby. Whisper is going to be just fine. He finally pooped, and he's been eating hay and turning it into manure like an absolute factory! Everything is back to normal!"

Shelby whooped a happy cry. "This is the best news ever, Rose! I'm so glad. I was so scared."

The girls spoke to each other in loud, excited tones as Rose explained how they had had a rough, terrifying night, but Whisper had finally started feeling better around sunrise.

"Dad and I are going home now to sleep, but unless something happens, we're going to be back in a couple of hours. Katherine's going to come out later, too, if you want to ride with her," Rose explained.

"I can hear her from here," Shelby's dad said from his desk. "Yes, you can go with Katherine." He waved his hand. "I guess we're not going to sleep in today. I'll go make coffee." He stood up and wandered off like a zombie.

Shelby was already waiting in the driveway when Drew and Katherine pulled up later that afternoon. Both girls were extremely anxious to see Rose and Whisper. Even Drew seemed a little on edge, going just a little faster than he usually did.

In fact, when they arrived at the barn, he drove past the main entrance and directly to the outdoor entrance to Aisle E. The entire Jensen family—including the twins—were gathered there.

Katherine and Shelby flew out of the car before Drew had completely stopped, and Rose came running towards them. They met in a giant hug.

"I was so scared," Rose said. Her face was red and swollen, and Shelby could tell she had been crying. "But he's going to be ok!"

The girls went into the barn, where Whisper was standing in his stall, happily munching hay. *If I didn't know better, I'd say this horse was perfectly fine,* Shelby thought.

"Whispie, you nerd," Katherine addressed the horse while patting the side of his neck. "Don't you ever do that to us again!"

Rose explained, "Dr. Iver said it wasn't super bad colic, but it was far enough along that Shelby got here at just the right time. You saved my horse's life, Shelby!"

Shelby was shocked. "You-you don't know that," she stammered. "Most colic cases resolve themselves." She was quoting from the lesson workbook now.

Rose shook her head. "I don't need to know about the what-ifs. What I know is that my horse colicked, and my friend Shelby Simone did all the right things to make sure he had the best chance of surviving." Rose folded Shelby into another big hug. Shelby could barely breathe, but she decided she would be pretty emotional if her horse was sick, too, and hugged Rose back.

Rose's parents came over and joined in the hug. Shelby had never been part of a group hug before, but this seemed ok. Sheriff Jensen and Mrs. Jensen looked like they had been crying, too.

"Whisper is part of the family, Shelby, and you just helped out our family in a time of need. We really appreciate that. Really. Can't tell you how much it means." Sheriff Jensen looked like he could use a few more hours of sleep.

"Shelby, I can't tell you how happy we are that it was you who happened to be there for Whisper. Rose tells me you really know your stuff. She brought home those books of yours, and I didn't know…" Mrs. Jensen trailed off. Rose explained that her mom had driven all night with the twins when she found out how serious Whisper's colic had been.

Shelby felt intense heat as her face flushed what she assumed was an extra-deep shade of red. "It wasn't anything. I just noticed him." She gestured vaguely at where Whisper had been lying when she first saw him. "I just did what I was supposed to do. Besides, you should be mad at me for walking your horse without your permission."

"Mad at you?" Rose yelped loudly, and her parents made hush noises at her. "Mad at you?" Rose said again, this time in a much lower voice. "I don't care if you walk my horse to the moon. I trust you to do whatever you want!"

Shelby felt relieved. "I swear I won't go around just taking horses for a walk," she said, mostly towards Bill. "But walking Whisper was the only thing I could think of doing while I waited for Bill and Dr. Iver."

"And that was some good quick thinking, Shelby," Bill added. "I'm sorry I jumped on you for that when I found you. I was just so worried about Whisper that I didn't bother to check myself. I know you're smart enough not to get yourself into major trouble, but I just reacted."

"In fact," he continued, "I'm going to make sure every horse in the barn is fine with being handled by other people. I'm also going to make sure there's a halter and lead rope on every stall door. Something like this could happen any time, and I want to make sure that quick thinkers like Shelby can get in there and save the day." He winked at Shelby. "What do you say you help me with that project, Shelby? Got anything going on next week?"

Shelby beamed a huge smile. "Nothing at all." She looked at Katherine. "Mind if I hitch a ride?"

Katherine grinned widely. "I think we'll have room for you in the car next week."

Rose also smiled. "I'm going to be here hand-walking Whisper, too. He has to be on a special diet and exercise plan to make sure he doesn't have another colic while he heals."

Shelby frowned. "But your vacation!"

Sheriff Jensen shook his head. "There will be other times. Plus, we can always head up there on the weekends. The best part of owning a lake house is that you can always visit. Maybe we'll take you girls and your families up there before the summer is through."

"But before we all go home and go back to bed, I wanted to make sure you had this," Mrs. Jensen said to Shelby. Bill handed her an envelope.

Inside the envelope was a thank-you card with flowers all over it. Shelby pulled out the card and opened it. Not only had Rose and Mrs. Jensen written long thankful messages to Shelby in it but there was a little piece of purple paper inside. Shelby turned it over. It read:

"This Certificate Entitles the Bearer to $300 Credit at The Old Quarry Lake Tack Shop. Signed, Marian Coolidge, Owner."

The message was handwritten in marker, and Shelby suspected that Bill had just returned from running a quick errand back to the feed shop, which shared a building with Marian's tack shop.

"I can't take this," Shelby said, shaking her head. "I just did what anyone would do."

"Don't worry, then," Sheriff Jensen said. "I would make sure anyone was rewarded for their actions. I just might not get anyone a gift card to their favorite tack shop. Now, if you'll all excuse us, the Jensen Family Circus is going to pack up and spend the rest of the day asleep. Bill?" He looked at the trainer wearily.

Bill tipped his cowboy hat. "I think we're in the clear for now, Sheriff. Get home and rest. I'll keep an eye on the big guy, and I think I can find some helpers, too." He nodded at Katherine and Shelby.

For the rest of the afternoon, Shelby and Katherine helped out with all of the chores in Aisle E. They swept the tack room. They picked out the stalls and swept the aisleway. They even dumped, scrubbed, and refilled all the water buckets. As Dr. Iver had stressed, horses needed to drink plenty of water to avoid colicking. Whisper cooperated by continuing to turn hay into manure.

Before they knew it, Drew had arrived to pick them up again. As they drove back to Shelby's house, Katherine turned to Shelby. "You are a hero, you know," she said matter-of-factly.

"No..." Shelby started, but Katherine held up her hand to shush her.

"You are a hero. Trust me. My dad works in the emergency room, and we've heard stories. Do you think just anyone would know what to do in that situation? Do you think Thomas would have thought to call Bill, the vet, and hand-walk Whisper? Do you think Thomas would have even cared?"

Shelby thought about it. "Well, he was in the same colic lesson I was in."

"That doesn't mean he was learning anything. He spent the whole time trying to turn his worksheet into a paper airplane," Katherine rolled her eyes. "And he didn't even do that right. He ended up ripping it and throwing it away."

Shelby laughed. Somehow that seemed like a very Thomas thing to do.

"Besides, we all know it's one thing to know about something and another to go ahead and do it. Our dad is always telling us about folks who come into the ER, and no one thought to do the Heimlich Maneuver on them or whatever. They know how to, but they just don't."

"They just choke," Drew said, laughing at what he clearly felt was a very witty joke.

"Ignore that nerd," Katherine said. "But the point is, other people might have freaked out, or just thought Whisper was sleeping. You paid attention to the symptoms, jumped into action, and now Whisper is going to be just fine. And don't give me that *anybody* stuff because nobody else was there. It was just you, Shelby. You saved the day."

Shelby's Diary

Diary, can you believe it? I'm a hero.

I still don't know what that means. Everyone is saying I saved Whisper's life, but I wasn't trying to be special or anything. I was just doing what I knew needed to be done.

I feel so bad for Rose and her family. Her parents had horses when they were growing up. It's a family thing to have horses, even though Sheriff Jensen is currently busy with Sheriff stuff, and Mrs. Jensen has her hands full with the twins. But they all love Whisper so much.

And Diary, Whisper wasn't a cheap horse, either. Rose was telling us about how much training he has had. She really wants to show him and go places, and they're both talented enough to do it, too! Anyway, I just can't imagine what would have happened if he wasn't fine. It's so scary how delicate horses are!

Rose's family gave me a gift card to Marian's tack shop in town. It was just a handwritten piece of paper, so I think it's something the Sheriff, Bill, and Marian came up with together. It's a really big amount, Diary. Think, like, five pairs of riding pants!

I guess horse camp was more monumental than I expected, Diary. I mean, I knew about colic before from books, but now I know what it looks like!

But then the whole Thomas thing. And riding Buddy. And learning how to post the trot. I need to try that on Coins again to see if I can. It's going to be sad riding just once a week now, after riding twice a day. I don't think I'll forget about the posting trot, though. It's just like Bill and Katherine and Rose told me– you've got to let the horse move you. It's just one of those things where you don't get it until you get it, Diary.

I guess a lot of things are like that, actually.

Anyway, Diary. It has been a long day and a long summer, and that's not including the bonus weeks we're about to get. Time to get some shut-eye, as Bill would say!

Chapter Eleven

Saying Farewell to the Summer

"Okay, so what's this about Thomas trying to say no one else can ride Buddy?" Rose asked. "What kind of weird things happened at camp?"

Katherine and Shelby laughed and rolled their eyes at the same time. "What a little punk!" Katherine exclaimed. "He couldn't take the fact that Shelby can ride Buddy just as well as he can, so his dad told Bill that only Thomas can ride Buddy going forward."

"So does that mean they bought him?" Shelby asked. She would miss riding Buddy, but not that much. She still had a lot to learn from Coins.

The girls were gathered in Shelby's room. This time, the girls had convinced Dr. Simone to let them order pizza, and a giant banana pepper and pineapple pie was on its way to Shelby and Katherine from Pasquale's. Rose and Shelby's parents were eating what they called, "a pepperoni pizza for the less adventurous."

"That's the thing," Katherine shook her head in disbelief as she rolled over on Shelby's bed. "Thomas doesn't actually want to buy Buddy. He just wants to make sure no one else rides him. It doesn't make sense."

"So, what did Bill say?" Rose asked. She was squished up in a beanbag chair, flipping through one of Shelby's horsebooks.

"Exactly that. He told them both that the only way to make sure a horse wasn't used in lessons was to take over ownership and sign a form that Buddy couldn't be used in the lesson program."

Rose nodded. "We did that with Whisper when we first got him. We weren't sure how he would react to other riders, but he's doing great with Brianne and some of the other older girls, so we might change that."

"Right. I actually chose to let Comet be ridden in lessons, but no one likes riding her slow self," Katherine said with a sigh.

"I would like to ride her slow self," Shelby said wistfully. "But I'm not nearly good enough for that," she quickly finished. She tried to look very interested in tidying up the top of her desk to hide her embarrassment.

"Sure, you are," Katherine said with a grin. "She's like Coins, only she won't save you if you zone out. She'll start jogging until you wake up. But anyway, I want to get into this whole Buddy thing."

According to Katherine, Thomas's father had offered to purchase Buddy. "Bill told him with a straight face that Buddy was priceless," she said. "But Thomas's dad wouldn't hear it, so he asked Bill to name a price."

"Did he?" Shelby was shocked.

Katherine nodded, "But guess what it was. $100,000!" She squealed and giggled.

"For a prehistoric lesson horse? That's hilarious!" Rose giggled, too. Even as a newcomer, Shelby knew that was a ridiculously high number for an elderly horse with a show record that was older than Thomas himself.

"But apparently, they're in the market to get Thomas a horse now, so he can join the show team," Katherine rolled her eyes again. "Good luck with that, I guess."

Rose spoke up next. "So, we now need to decide what we're doing for the last days of summer."

"Shelby's gonna ride Comet," Katherine said. "And then we have that three-day weekend with your family at the lake house. Your dad's going to show me how to fish."

Shelby objected. "I'm not nearly good enough to ride Comet!"

"Shelby's gonna ride Comet," Katherine repeated. "Because if my nerd brother can ride Comet, so can Superhero Shelby!"

Just then, the girls heard a rustle by the front door. The Simone's farmhouse had screen doors at the front and back, so the family left them open as much as possible for the fresh air. Shelby didn't think she'd ever experienced so much fresh air in her life since their condo in the city didn't even have opening windows.

It was Sid Pasquale, bringing their pizza. *That's another thing that's different from the city,* Shelby thought. *The pizza place's owner doesn't usually do his own deliveries in the city!*

As the girls filed downstairs, Dr. Simone met them in the den with plates, utensils, drinks, and napkins. After all, she couldn't miss an episode of Swann Johnson's adventures.

Shelby rolled her eyes but smiled. Old Quarry Lake sure was different from the city, but it was pretty OK, she thought.

Shelby's Diary

Diary, can you believe everything that has happened in the past couple of months? Remember not that long ago, when I wrote in the city? On my desk overlooking Broad Street? How the city lights would keep my room from getting too dark, and I'd read books all night from the light coming in through those big windows?

I can't do that here in Old Quarry Lake, Diary. It's too dark at night. No lights outside. But the stars are super-duper bright out here.

I've been thinking about how much things have changed this summer. Katherine and Rose came over for dinner and Swann Johnson and Uno, and we had pizza, even though Mom always tries not to. None of that was happening just a few months ago. Maybe Amy and Jackie would come over for a sleepover, but we usually got takeout Chinese and watched movies on Netflix or whatever.

I'm really glad I met Katherine and Rose. It's even better that they're my horse friends, but I think we would still be friends even if we didn't have horses. The horses just make it that much better.

School's going to start soon, too. I'll know Katherine and Rose, but everyone else is going to know that I'm the New Girl. And I won't know who they are. Still, at least I've got my buddies.

Plus, I don't have to worry about that for a little bit longer, Diary. And I'm really looking forward to going to the lake with the Jensens. The only lake I've been to was the Great Salt Lake in Utah, and I know that's not the norm for lakes. Especially not in the Appalachian foothills!

Anyway, I think one thing is clear, Diary: Shelby Simone is officially a horse person. Horse girl, I guess. But that's not a bad thing.

In fact, it's a very, very, very, very, very-times-infinity good thing!

Glossary

Shelby's Horse Terms

There are so many words to remember in the horse world! Shelby thought to herself. She looked up at her many bookshelves of beloved horse books with a grin. *So many words,* she thought again, this time thrilled at the idea of a challenge.

Shelby's dad loved words. He was always using unfamiliar words and challenging her to look them up in the dictionary, and they loved playing the Thesaurus Game together. That's where they took turns using words that meant something similar until they ran out.

At the same time, he tended to trip over a lot of the words that the girls used when talking about horses. She didn't blame him. A halter and a bridle looked a lot alike if you didn't know what they were used for.

Shelby had an idea—what if she came up with a list of the horse terms she and her friends used all the time? She could share it with her mom and dad, and maybe her friends would want to share it with their parents, as well. Then they could follow along when Shelby and her friends went off on their long horse-related tales. While they might not memorize all the words, at least they could have a friendly guide to help them follow along!

We could probably give one to Drew, too, Shelby thought. She frowned immediately. *He probably wouldn't read it, though.* Then the frown changed to a smile. *Well, he probably would, but he wouldn't admit it.*

She got started by jotting down all the horse terms she could think of, and what they meant. Maybe she'd make a few extra notes so they could understand when to use the terms, too. After all, she couldn't expect her parents to devote as much time to researching horses as she had.

She booted up her computer and started typing. *This is going to be quite the project,* Shelby thought. *But definitely worth it. I bet Mom and Dad and the girls are going to love it!*

Shelby's Horse Terms

Parts of the Horse
In the Barn
Getting Ready
Working with the Horse
Disciplines

Parts of the Horse

There are way too many horse parts to list here. A lot of them are obvious, like eyes, ears, and nostrils. A lot of them we don't think about too often. Here are some of the parts of the horse that are important, but not so obvious.

Barrel - The widest part of a horse's tummy. This includes most of the horse's ribcage area between the front legs and the back legs. This is where the girth of the saddle goes, so it's important to make sure this area is clean and not chafed.

Cannon Bone - The short bone that runs from a horse's knee to the hoof. This is where a lot of leg wraps and performance boots are placed. This is also one of the most delicious places for insects to bite and one of the most fragile spots on the horse's body. Lots of veins, tendons, and ligaments run up close to the bone here.

Crest - The top of a horse's neck. This is where the mane grows. It's also a great place for wrapping arms around when hugging a horse, and lots of horses appreciate scratching or rubbing along the crest.

Digestive system - Horses have really delicate digestive systems that are designed to graze all the time. Their long necks are perfect for reaching a variety of food sources, and they actually have very small stomachs. They also have a really long, complicated network of intestines. Since horses can't throw up, having a tummy ache or intestinal trouble can be a really big deal for a horse. Digestive problems in a horse usually mean a *colic* episode.

Forelock - Most horses grow a long tuft of hair between their ears. When working with a horse, it's a good idea to make sure the forelock is out of the horse's eyes and doesn't get tangled in their bridle. You can actually use clippers to remove the area where the forelock and mane meet by the ears. The shaved area is called a *bridlepath*.

Hoof - Made of the same stuff as human fingernails, called *keratin*. Horse hooves look pretty basic, but many bones, tendons, ligaments, and blood vessels help horses run fast and gracefully.

Fun Fact: Have you ever seen a frog on a horse? If you get a chance to pick up a horse's hoof, you will. The frog is the spongey v-shaped part of the bottom of a hoof. It helps with circulation, balance, and shock absorption.

Poll - This is the bony spot between a horse's ears, where the spine and the skull meet. A bridle and halter put pressure on the horse's poll, among other spots on a horse's face, to help control them.

Tail - This one is kind of obvious, but it's important to know that a horse's tail is actually part of their spine. There are an average of 18 vertebrae—spinal column bones—in a horse's tail!

Withers - This is the knobby area where a horse's neck and back meet at the top of their shoulders.

Fun Fact: A horse's height is measured from the top of their withers to the ground. The unit of measurement for horses is called hands. One hand equals four inches. So, if someone says a horse is 15 hands high, that means they're 60 inches tall, or 5 feet tall.

If a particular critter is 14.2 hands high or taller, they are officially a horse. If they are under 14.2 hands, they are considered a pony!

The Barn

Barns are filled with lots of equipment for horses and riders, plus tools to maintain the structure itself. These are some of the areas, tools, and equipment that horse people may work with regularly.

Aisleway - Some barns are designed with rows of stalls that open onto a main hallway. In a barn, that hall is called the "aisle" or the "aisleway." It's important to keep the aisleway clean and clear of equipment so that it's safe for horses and people to walk through.

Arena - This is where the magic happens! An arena is any area sectioned off specifically for working with horses. An indoor arena has walls and a roof. A covered arena just has a roof. An outdoor arena may have a fence around it, but it doesn't necessarily have to.

Bedding - This is what goes in a horse's stall to absorb their messes. Bedding should also provide a cushiony surface for horses to stand on and usually adds a little warmth, too. Wood shavings are commonly used as bedding, but it's important to know that black walnut is toxic to horses. Straw or straw pellets are also popular.

Cross ties - Cross ties are frequently found in the *aisleway* or *wash rack* and are used to keep horses standing still while people work with them. A long rope or chain is fastened to the wall. At the end of the rope or chain is a clip. The clip is attached to a loop on a horse's halter. Typically, there's one tie on each side of the horse, so they're "cross" tied.

Footing - This is what the *arena* floor is covered with. Different barns use different types of footing to make sure the horses have enough support for the activities they're doing and the weather they have.

Grain (also called Feed) - Not all horses eat grain! Grain helps supplement a horse's nutritional needs if they can't get it all through grass and hay. Some of them have special ingredients to help horses with health issues.

Halter - This is a combination of straps, rings, buckles, and snaps that go around a horse's head. A halter works a lot like a dog's collar. The rings on each side of the horse's face can be clipped to cross ties. Lead ropes and lunge lines can be connected to the ring under the horse's chin, like snapping a leash on a dog's collar.

Hay - This is what makes up most of a horse's daily food. Hay is basically dried grass, but the process is a little more complex than leaving lawn clippings out. If the hay gets too wet during the process, it may be impossible for horses to eat it because of their *digestive system*.

Fun Fact: Horses should eat about 2% of their body weight in hay, so a horse who weighs 1000 pounds would need 20 pounds of hay every day to keep their digestive systems working properly and give them the nutrients they need.

Lead rope - This is a rope that's about 3-5 feet in length and clips to a horse's halter. It's mainly used for leading a horse safely from one spot to another.

Lunge line - This is a rope that's usually 25-35 feet in length. It can clip to a halter, bridle, or special equipment for lunging a horse.

Fun Fact: "Lunging a horse" means making them work in circles around a person who is holding on to the other end of the rope. Lunging can be used in training a horse or rider, exercising a horse who's feeling a little zany (like Whisper), or when helping a horse recover from an injury.

Mats - Rubber mats can be found in many different places in a barn- inside *stalls*, in *aisleways,* and even in *tack rooms*. They are easy to clean and provide extra cushioning.

Mucking - Cleaning a stall. Horse stalls need to be mucked pretty much every day so horses aren't standing in their own mess. That can be bad for their hooves, skin, and breathing.

Stall - A horse's own apartment! Stalls typically have walls, a roof, and at least one door to let them in and out. Some horses live in a stall all day, while others come in only to sleep. Some horses have never been in a stall at all!

Tack - All of the supplies that go into horse keeping, including *halters, lead ropes, lunging* equipment, *saddles, bridles, girths, saddle pads, blankets,* and more are considered "tack."

Tack Room- This is an area where the *tack* is kept. Sometimes it's an actual room, and other times it's more of a general area in a barn where equipment can be safely stored out of the way. Some really fancy barns have temperature-controlled tack rooms, which helps keep leather goods at the right temperature and humidity.

Tack Shop and Feed Mill- Basically, businesses that sell horse equipment and feed. There are many different types of horse equipment though, so some stores will carry different items:
- Sometimes a tack shop only sells rider apparel and tack.
- Some sell home decorations, toys, and other fun gifts, but not a whole lot of practical day-to-day stuff.
- Sometimes a tack shop will be near or include a feed mill, which is a store that sells grain and other horse food, like hay pellets and dietary supplements.

- Sometimes a feed mill will sell a few extra horse accessories, like *halters* and *grooming* supplies.

It's totally confusing at first, but usually, each shop shares what they carry on their social media or website.

Wash rack - This is an area specifically designed for washing horses, with a floor that drains and a water source. A lot of barns make sure the wash rack floor has extra texture or *mats* to prevent horses from slipping.

Whip - There are lots of different types of whips used when working with horses. Some are short and used to give a horse a tap on the neck to get their attention. Others are longer and used behind the leg when riding to tell a horse that you really want them to move forward. Lunge whips and driving whips are even longer so that they can reach horses who are being lunged or driven.

It's super-important to know that whips aren't meant to hurt horses. Mainly they're used like a friendly wave or poke to get a horse's attention.

Getting Ready

This is where the horse world gets really interesting! Depending on what someone does with their horse, they may or may not have all of these things in their barn. They may also have lots of things mentioned here– these are just some of the basics for someone getting started in riding lessons or just lurking around the barn.

Bit - This is the part of a bridle that goes in a horse's mouth. While every part of the *bridle* has a purpose in controlling a horse's head movement, the bit is connected directly to the hand motion of the person riding or driving the horse through the *reins*. A horse's mouth is pretty sensitive, so it's important to be kind and flexible with your hand movements.

Blankets - Horses wear blankets for a lot of different reasons. A lot of times, blankets are used in the colder months to keep horses from getting too cold or wet, but these aren't the only reasons. Some blankets are designed to keep horses clean before a big show. Some blankets are designed to keep a horse's coat and skin from getting wet or muddy. Others can protect from bugs and the sun.

Bridle - Like a *halter*, a bridle is a bunch of straps and buckles, designed to be worn around the horse's head. However, a bridle usually includes a *bit* and a set of *reins*. Together, a bridle, bit, and reins help riders or drivers communicate a bunch of different things to the horse, like how fast or slow to go, where to turn, and when to stop.

Body brush - This is a type of brush used for whisking dirt and bedding off of a horse's coat. It kind of looks and acts like a broom, sweeping the horse's body clean.

Boots and wraps - Different types of leg coverings are used to protect a horse's legs, especially the *cannon bone*. Different types of boots and wraps do different things, such as protecting a horse from hitting its front legs with its back feet or supporting the many important tendons and ligaments that run from the horse's knee to its *hoof*.

Clipping - This basically involves shaving down part of a horse's body with a pair of heavy horse clippers. These look just like the set you might see at a barber shop but made to clip through a horse's heavy coat, mane, and tail.

Fun Fact: Horses can be clipped for lots of reasons. Keeping them cool and dry in the winter is a popular reason since horses who grow a thick winter coat will sweat a lot when they work hard. *Clipping them allows areas that get really hot to stay dry so they can stay in training year-round. Some breeds also require horses to be groomed to a certain standard in the show ring, which can involve clipping a horse's ears and chin whiskers. Clipping can also help horses who are healing from skin irritation problems.*

Curry comb - This type of brush is designed with little teeth that help grind dried mud and heavy dirt out of a horse's coat. It's used in a circular motion in the direction of the horse's coat and gives the horse a little massage while you brush them!

Girth - This is a strap that goes around a horse's *barrel* to keep the *saddle* in place. Different types of girths are used for different types of saddles. They can even fasten in different ways!

Fun Fact: Some horses hold their breath when their bellies are at their largest to avoid pinching from the girth. That's why it's a good idea to slowly tighten a girth. You may have to check the girth several times when tacking up and even after mounting up. If the girth is too loose, the saddle may slide around on the horse's back, which can be uncomfortable for the horse and dangerous for the rider.

Grooming - Before *tacking up* for a work session, many people groom their horses. This helps them make sure their horses are free from any irritating dirt where the saddle, girth, and boots or wraps may be. A basic grooming session includes using a curry comb, body brush, and hoof pick. It's also a good chance to check the horse over for any small injuries or discomfort that you might not see unless you're that close!

Harness - A harness is a specific system of straps, buckles, snaps, and loops for a driving horse. There are different types of harnesses for different types of driving, like pulling a cart or carriage, dragging heavy loads and farm equipment, and working in muddy or snowy weather.

Hoof pick - This is a hook-shaped tool that's used to clean mud, manure, rocks, and *bedding* out of a horse's *hoof*.

Fun Fact: Cleaning a horse's hooves is called "picking hooves" because of this tool. Sometimes a coach or instructor will say "Be sure to pick his hooves out," or "Did you remember to pick her hooves?" They want to make sure there isn't any potential debris in a horse's hoof which could make it uncomfortable or cause bruising.

Reins - The reins are long straps that connect from the bit to the rider or driver's hands. Different *disciplines* use different *bits*, *bridles*, and *reins*. This means that the movement of the reins can send very different messages to different horses based on their training.

Saddle - Different *disciplines* use saddles that help riders get into the right position for that style of riding. *Western* saddles have a horn and deep seat that were originally developed as tools for cowboys and other long-distance and wilderness riders. *English* saddles have a flatter, simpler design that helps riders get off a horse's back when jumping and are more lightweight. Riders in higher levels of competition often have saddles designed specifically for the demands of their discipline. Don't worry—there's a whole section about disciplines with more information about that part!

Fun Fact: While saddles are traditionally made of leather, some modern saddles are made out of synthetic products that are more lightweight and easier to care for than leather saddles.

Saddle pad - Different types of padding can be used under a saddle to make it more comfortable for the horse. Some saddle pads provide a little cushion and sweat absorption, while others help the saddle fit better. Some help make sure a rider's weight is correctly distributed across the horse's spine.

Stirrup - Where riders put their feet (unless it's a no-stirrups lesson). Many different types of stirrups can be used, depending on the *saddle* and *discipline*. *Fun fact: Specialty stirrups exist for good reasons.* Some stirrups are designed to help riders with knee, ankle, and hip pain. Some are designed to keep a rider's leg in a certain position. Some even snap open in case of an accident!

Stirrup leather - This is a long strap of leather that the stirrup dangles from. Most saddles are designed with a bar or other type of permanent fastener which the stirrup leather wraps around. The leather has many different holes in it that allow riders to adjust how long their stirrups are.

Tacking up - The process of getting a horse ready for work. Whether that involves a *saddle* or *harness*, tacking up means getting all of the equipment on the horse so that it's ready to go into the arena and work.

Working with the Horse

This part can be tricky because there are a lot of different ways to work with horses. Horses can be ridden, driven, used for farm work, or do different activities with a human who is on the ground. These are called different *disciplines*, and we'll get into the details about what those are in their own section.

But there are a few terms used when working with horses that are important for all horse people to learn.

Bareback - This is when someone rides a horse without a saddle. Usually, they still use a *bridle* or *halter* and *lead rope* to help them communicate with their horse.

Fun fact: A horse's back is surprisingly slippery to sit on. Plus, a horse's back moves in all sorts of different directions when they walk, so you'll get a pretty good tummy and hip workout when you ride bareback!

Breeches and riding tights - Technically, the term *breeches* refers to pants worn by English-discipline riders. These pants are form-fitting, like leggings, and have a waistband that fastens. That sounds weirdly specific, but riding tights are even more like leggings because they're pull-on style, meaning they don't have a snap or zipper.

Fun Fact: Breeches and riding tights usually have a grippy knee patch that provides extra protection from slipping in the saddle. Full-seat breeches and tights have a grippy patch or material applied from the mid-calf all the way up to the bottom area. That helps riders have even better contact in the saddle.

Buck - A true buck involves a horse putting their head down and raising their back legs and kicking outward. Bucks can be little or big enough to lift the entire horse off the ground! Usually, horses buck to let humans know they're in pain or feel threatened.

Chaps and half-chaps - These types of leg protection are usually made out of leather or a similar grippy material. They can not only keep riders from getting chafed but also keep their legs in place and quiet on the saddle so they can communicate with the horse better.

Cues - Since humans can't speak horse, we communicate with them through a series of cues. Riding cues can include pressure on the *reins*, sitting deeper in the *saddle*, or tapping a horse with a *whip*. Horses are taught cues to lead politely on a *lead rope*, to work on the *lunge line*, or to pull a cart or other equipment, too.

Fun Fact: Horses are pretty smart, so they can be taught all sorts of different cues. Since they're prey animals, they have a really good read on body language, which can be helpful when training them with different cues.

Some cues are vocal, like saying "Whoa." Horses can even pick up on different tones of "Whoa" to know when their handler means business. Some cues are physical, like nudging a horse with your heels to go forward or pulling back on the reins to ask them to stop or slow down. Horses can also pick up on really subtle cues, like whistles, clicks, and hand position.

Dismounting - The process of getting off of the horse. It seems complicated at first, but you basically pivot on your left foot while swinging your right leg over the horse's back. You've just got to lean forward and find your balance point so you can do it nice and slowly!

Gaits - Humans can walk, run, skip, hop, and move at different speeds and rhythms. Horses can do the same thing—we call them gaits. The main four gaits are *walk*, *trot*, *canter*, and *gallop*. Some horses are referred to as "gaited" because they have extra ways of moving. For more details on gaited horses, check out breeds like the Tennessee Walking Horse, Missouri Fox Trotter, or Rocky Mountain Horse.

Walk - This is a horse's slowest gait. The walk is a four-beat gait, meaning each hoof lands on the ground in sequence.

Trot - The trot is usually a lot faster than the walk, and a lot bumpier, too. That's because when trotting, a horse's front and rear diagonal legs are moving at the same time. The horse's front right and left rear legs will move at the same time, and the front left and right rear legs will move at the same time.

Fun Fact: There are two main ways to ride the trot. A sitting trot means you're letting your backside sit in the saddle, following the side-to-side and front-to-back motion of the horse's back. You can also try the posting trot, which means rising out of the saddle when the horse's outside leg goes forward. In the saddle, you can actually see the horse's shoulder go forward. It takes a while to find the rhythm and build the muscles needed to do the posting trot really well!

Canter - Even faster than the trot, a canter has three beats. When a horse is cantering, one front leg moves further in front of the horse than the others to help them keep their balance when turning. The leg that moves forward further is called a horse's lead— a horse is either on their left lead or their right lead.

Gallop - This is generally a horse's fastest gait. The horse's legs move in a rapid four-beat pattern that allows the horse to stretch their full body length so they can cover as much ground and move as quickly as possible.

Heels down - This is something that riding coaches and instructors say at least a million times a day. A lot of riding cues involve movement from the seat and legs. Having your heels down can not only help you find a more solid position but improves your balance, as well. Plus, it helps with shock absorption in our ankles and knees.

Helmet - Riding helmets are specifically designed to protect the skull and brain during a potential horseback riding accident. Many riding facilities require kids to wear them whenever they're around or on a horse.

Mounting up - This is the art of getting on a horse. While some tall, flexible, strong people can reach their left foot from the ground to the stirrup and jump up, riding barns will have mounting blocks, which are little steps, ladders, or other tall, flat, solid surfaces a rider can use to help them mount up.

On the flat - The flat is just the ground. When someone is riding on the flat, they aren't going over any jumps or dealing with obstacles. At shows, the classes that don't have jumps, obstacles, or specific tests are called "flat classes."

Over fences - This is another term for *jumping*. There are several different types of jumping, which we'll get to in the Disciplines section. But when someone says they're working or showing over fences, they mean they're working on jumping.

Rear - When a horse puts all their weight on their rear legs and lifts their front legs in the air, it's called rearing. A horse usually rears for the same reason it *bucks*: because it feels threatened or uncomfortable.

School - Not only is this a big building where people learn, but it's what we call it when we're working with a horse on a particular skill. If someone says they're *schooling trot transitions*, that means they're having a study session with their horse to practice that particular movement.

Spook - It's called "spooking" because the horse is reacting to something that scared them. This is usually a very fast sideways, forward, backward, or up-and-down motion that isn't always easy to follow if you're sitting in the saddle.

Fun Fact: All kinds of things can make a horse spook. Loud, sudden noises are common, which is why most barns ask that people be quiet and use their indoor voices when working with horses. Horses can also think that something moving very quickly is a threat, so it's a good idea to move slowly and let horses know that you are present by greeting them or patting them as you walk past them. This gets their attention and lets them know you're not a scary predator at the same time.

Horses can also spook at things they've seen every day, like the squeaky door on their stall or their own shadow.

- **Steering** - This is how we tell the horse where to go. We mostly use our hand and *rein* position to move the *bit*, which tells the horse's head where to go. You can also use your legs to tell the horse's *barrel* and rear end where to go. Riders at really high levels can even *cue* their horses to steer based on their balance!

- **Transitions** - This is what we call a change in *gait*. Going from the walk to the trot or from the canter to the trot uses different muscles in both the horse and rider, so practicing transitions can help both horse and rider gain balance and strength.

Disciplines

In the horse world, we call the different sports and activities we do with our horses "disciplines." Just like when trying different types of dancing or different events in track and field, each equine discipline requires its own set of skills, knowledge, and equipment.

Most disciplines can be categorized into "English" or "Western," based on the type of *saddle* and *tack* used.

- **English** - We call these disciplines "English" because of the type of tack typically used in that activity. Way back in the 1700s, European riders were interested in saddles that had a deeper seat. They used these saddles for combat, travel, and farm work, which meant they had to be comfortable and easy to mount and dismount.

  As racing, fox-hunting, and other competitive types of riding became popular across Europe, the saddles were redesigned to allow riders to follow the motion of the horse and help both the horse and rider do their job better. As these sports spread around the world, the "English" saddles and bridles became part of the discipline.

There are many different English disciplines, but a few examples include:

Dressage - Also developed in the 1700s, dressage asks a horse and rider to use their balance, strength, and agility to complete a pattern. These patterns—called dressage tests—can include walk, trot, canter, and transitions between the gaits. There are also a few sideways moves that might be required—we call these *lateral moves* in the horse world. In competition, the horse and rider are judged by how well they move through these tests.

Fun Fact: Dressage technically isn't just an English sport, though. Western dressage is a pretty new discipline, but quickly gaining in popularity.

Eventing - Also called three-day eventing, this type of competition has three phases. Riders show their horses in a dressage test, over jumps in a ring for the Stadium phase, and at a full gallop while navigating obstacles and jumping outdoors in what's called the Cross-Country phase. Not only do riders have to be good at the three different disciplines, but the Stadium and Cross-Country phases are timed, so they have to be fast and accurate.

Hunters - While many equine sports are based on having the fastest time, hunter classes are judged more like dressage—style counts! Both on the *flat* and *over fences*, hunter horses and ponies are expected to show a clean, crisp form and make their jobs look super easy.

Saddleseat - Very technically speaking, saddleseat saddles are their own thing, but a lot of horse shows still group these riders with the English sports. Saddleseat horses are usually *gaited*, and the classes are usually designed so that judges can score the horses and riders on their movement and style.

Show Jumping - This is a timed event *over fences*, but style does still matter. Sort of. Horse and rider teams are penalized if they knock down any of the jumps. Even if one of the poles that makes up the jump is knocked down, they'll get a penalty. So, the goal of show jumping is to go "fast and clean"—as quickly as possible with no penalties. The fences get huge, and the patterns the teams are asked to ride can be really complicated, so fast and clean isn't always easy!

Western - The Western saddle has roots in work saddles all around the world, but many modern Western saddles are modeled after the saddles used in the American West in the 1800s.

The horn at the front of the saddle can be used as support for the rider, an anchor for a pulley or winch when used with ropes, or even a place to hang equipment and packs for carrying supplies. The saddle is designed to put riders in a more balanced, straight-legged position, which is helpful for many of the disciplines that traditionally use this type of saddle.

Sometimes, Western riders call the *trot* a "jog," and the *canter* a "lope." They are technically different since a jog and a lope are slower and less animated than the trot and canter English riders prefer, but the leg movements and hoof beats are the same.

Here are just a few Western disciplines:

Barrel Racing and Contesting - These are speed-based competitions in which horses and riders complete a specific pattern as quickly as possible. Barrel racing involves running a three-loop pattern around actual barrels. Pole-bending involves weaving around tall upright poles. There can be many different types of contesting classes at a show, but the main goal is to be super fast.

Cutting - This is one particular sport in which horses and riders work with cattle. Roping and sorting also involve horses moving cows. Typically, these events are timed, and horse and rider teams are asked to perform a certain task with a cow or small herd of cattle.

Fun Fact: Cowhorses are usually bred for these events because they have "cow sense." That means they know how to work with cattle and don't get scared by these strange, loud animals. Some cow horses seem to lock onto a cow and it looks like they know exactly what the cow is going to do.

Pleasure - Western Pleasure may be the slowest of the riding disciplines, but that's a good thing! Western Pleasure horses and riders show off their calm, smooth, slow gaits. A pleasure horse should look super comfortable to ride and as if you could spend all day riding the range together.

Reining - Some people compare reining to dressage, except it's a lot faster. Reining classes include patterns, just like dressage. Except in a reining class, horses and riders will be demonstrating their ability to ride loops, circles, and figure-eights at a canter and gallop. They're also asked to back up, come to an immediate stop, and even spin to demonstrate agility and balance.

Trail - You might think that trail riding is just for outside, but trail classes at shows let people show how their horses would navigate a pattern made out of common trail obstacles and challenges, like stepping over poles, walking forward, and backing up around obstacles, and even opening gates or moving equipment from one part of the arena to the other.

Fun Fact: Trail classes can be held "in hand," which means that handlers lead their horses from the ground. They may also be held "under saddle," which means horses will be ridden through the pattern.

Some disciplines welcome riders and handlers who are trained in either discipline or both! A few examples include:

Endurance - The name is a major hint about this sport. Endurance horses and riders hit the trail for long distances—sometimes even riding for multiple days to complete the course! All breeds and types of riding are welcome, though some endurance riders prefer *tack* and equipment made just for this sport.

Equitation - Instead of the horse being judged, this time it's the rider! The term "equitation" refers to the rider's effectiveness and poise while riding their horse. Since riding well is important to every discipline, shows will often have classes in English, Western, Saddleseat, and even bareback equitation.

Fun Fact: Most of the time, riders will be asked to memorize an equitation pattern the day of the show, then ask their horses to complete the pattern as accurately as possible. This might include transitions, circles, backing up, and stopping at certain spots around the arena. Since they won't know what the pattern is until they arrive at the show, equitation riders practice all sorts of movements, much like dressage riders.

Halter and Liberty - Also known as showmanship, halter sports are shown entirely in hand. That means that the handler works with the horse from the ground, communicating with a halter and lead rope. Liberty means no halter and lead rope—the handler communicates with the horse using hand signals, body language, voice, and sometimes a special whip or stick.

Shelby looked through her computer file for what must have been the hundredth time. "I think this looks good," she said out loud.

"What looks good, Sport?" her dad spoke behind her. She jumped at the sudden interruption.

"Dad! I didn't know you were there!" Shelby was a little out of breath from the scare. "I've been working on a guide to horse terms for you and Mom and, well, everyone who doesn't love horses as much as Katherine, Rose, Agate, and I do."

"I wondered what you've been doing. You've been down here in the den for hours. I was afraid the ugly carpet ate you!" Shelby's dad chuckled, even though he truly did hate the red den carpet.

"Why don't you take a look and tell me what you think?" Shelby looked up at her father, excited but just a little nervous. "Tell me what I missed?"

"Sounds good, Sport. Now go get ready for bed. Someone has to be at the barn bright and early tomorrow!" And with that, Shelby hugged her dad and climbed the stairs to start her bedtime routine.

Review

Reviews and feedback help improve this book and the author. If you enjoy this book, we would greatly appreciate it if you could take a few moments to share your opinion and post a review on Amazon. Thank you!

Exclusive Old Quarry Lake Farms Insider Info

Do you want to join Shelby Simone and her friends from Old Quarry Lake Farms on all their adventures?

Read about Shelby, Katherine, Rose, and all their pals in the Old Quarry Lake Farms Tales book series. Three girls who are wild about horses unite at their local town horse-riding stable. Together, they learn about horses, themselves, and what it means to be a good friend.

The Old Quarry Lake Farms Tales join a group of pre-teen girls who share a bond through horses. Together, they tackle situations like moving to a new town, feeling different, and accepting themselves and each other just as they are—while learning everything they can about horses!

Scan the code to join the Old Quarry Lake Farms email list and never miss out on Shelby's adventures. You'll gain access to bonus material, behind-the-scenes details, and sneak peeks at where Shelby's next steps will take her!

Please join My Facebook group

https://www.facebook.com/MartyKayJones

https://www.facebook.com/groups/881663880022320/

Made in United States
Troutdale, OR
06/07/2024

20401040R00084